NANCY MAHONEY

BASKET BONANZA

14 QUILTS FROM BEST-LOVED BLOCKS

Martingale®
& COMPANY

ACKNOWLEDGMENTS

A very special thank you to the staff at Martingale & Company, especially my technical editor, Ellen Pahl,
and my copy editor, Durby Peterson. I have enjoyed working with each and every one of you.
To Gretchen Engle, thank you for your machine quilting skills.
I am most grateful and appreciative of the following people and companies who have so generously given
their support and products for the projects in this book:

Clothworks and David Peha

P & B Textiles and Julie Scribner

Timeless Treasures and Emily Cohen

American & Efird and Marci Brier for Mettler and Signature threads

Hobbs Bonded Fibers and H. D. Wilbanks for batting

CREDITS

President: *Nancy J. Martin*

CEO: *Daniel J. Martin*

Publisher: *Jane Hamada*

Editorial Director: *Mary V. Green*

Managing Editor: *Tina Cook*

Technical Editor: *Ellen Pahl*

Copy Editor: *Durby Peterson*

Design Director: *Stan Green*

Illustrator: *Laurel Strand*

Cover and Text Designer: *Trina Craig*

Photographer: *Brent Kane*

That Patchwork Place® is an imprint of Martingale & Company®.

Basket Bonanza: 14 Quilts from Best-Loved Blocks
© 2005 by Nancy Mahoney

Martingale & Company
20205 144th Avenue NE
Woodinville, WA 98072-8478
www.martingale-pub.com

Printed in China
10 09 08 07 06 05   8 7 6 5 4 3 2 1

MISSION STATEMENT

*Dedicated to providing quality products and service
to inspire creativity.*

Library of Congress Cataloging-in-Publication Data

Mahoney, Nancy.
   Basket bonanza : 14 quilts from best-loved blocks / Nancy Mahoney.
      p. cm.
   ISBN 1-56477-555-0
   1. Patchwork—Patterns. 2. Quilting—Patterns. 3. Friendship quilts.
   4. Baskets in art. I. Title.
      TT835.M2715494. 2005
      746.46'041—dc22

                                    2004016001

C O N T E N T S

For many years I have enjoyed shopping for antiques, and I love the thrill of finding objects to add to my different collections. As a quilter, I found it natural to collect vintage quilts. I'm particularly fond of scrappy, traditional quilts, and those words describe many of the quilts in my collection.

One of my favorite quilts is a vintage basket quilt. This is the only quilt in my collection that is signed and dated. Even though the quilt has some stains, it is in remarkably good condition. I can't begin to express how excited I was to find this quilt, and I just had to have it.

In today's terminology, the quilt would be considered a friendship quilt. Each block is signed in permanent ink, and in one corner of the quilt is this inscription: "Lizzie Walker from Sister Maggie, June 9, 1884." Wouldn't you just love to know Lizzie Walker's story and how the quilt ended up in a shop in Seattle, Washington? Lizzie's quilt is wonderfully graphic and very typical of quilts from that period. You will find an updated version of the block from her quilt in "Spring Baskets" on page 54.

One hundred and twenty years after Lizzie's quilt was made, basket quilts and patterns are still among the best-loved patchwork designs. Their variety, versatility, and charm make them especially appealing to quilters. Baskets exemplify traditional patchwork designs.

Basket Bonanza features 14 beautiful patchwork quilts created from 13 different basket blocks. To further enhance the blocks, I've included them in a variety of settings—with dazzling results. For example, in "Baskets of Stars" (page 64), instead of the usual diagonal setting, I've arranged the basket blocks side by side in a straight set to create a striking secondary pattern.

I've also designed and included border variations that are quick and easy to piece using remarkably clever construction techniques. Borders provide the finishing touch to any quilt and have a dramatic effect on the overall appearance. For some quilts, a traditional plain border is the best choice, but a pieced border can be used to complement the blocks and turn a simple quilt into a stunning quilt. I hope you'll be eager to try some of these border treatments.

I have truly enjoyed designing and making the quilts for this book. Like most of you, I have broad tastes that change with my mood. I've tried to include a little something for everyone, from quilts with a traditional, heirloom design like "Nantucket Baskets" (page 23) to fun, easy quilts like "Picnic Baskets" (page 80), which is a perfect choice for large-scale novelty prints. I hope you will find many projects in this book to inspire you.

OPPOSITE: *Inscribed in the upper-right corner: "Lizzie Walker from Sister Maggie, June 9, 1884" (collection of Nancy Mahoney)*

On the pages that follow, you will find valuable information for the successful completion of your quilt. All of the quilts in this book use sew-and-trim techniques—you cut and sew with squares and rectangles; very few triangles are cut. This makes it much easier to be accurate and have successful results since you are not dealing with bias edges. Keep in mind that accuracy begins with careful cutting, precise sewing, and gentle pressing.

SUPPLIES

To make the quilts in this book, you will need the following supplies:

♦ 100%-cotton fabric as indicated for each quilt
♦ 100%-cotton thread
♦ Sewing machine in good working order
♦ Rotary-cutting equipment, including a rotary cutter, an 18" x 24" cutting mat, and a 6" x 24" acrylic ruler
♦ A 4" or 6" Bias Square® ruler, depending on the project you choose
♦ Fabric scissors
♦ Seam ripper
♦ Thin glass-head silk pins

ROTARY CUTTING

Instructions for rotary cutting are provided for all the quilts, and all measurements include ¼" seam allowances. If you are unfamiliar with rotary cutting, refer to Donna Lynn Thomas's *Shortcuts: A Concise Guide to Rotary Cutting* (Martingale & Company, 1999) for more detailed instructions.

Always remember that the blade of your rotary cutter is extremely sharp and you can cut yourself before you even notice. At all times keep the blade guard in place until you are ready to make a cut; then close the blade immediately after cutting. Keep your rotary cutter in a safe place, away from children and pets, when it is not in use.

Cutting Strips

Cutting strips at an exact right angle to the folded edge of your fabric is essential for accuracy. Rotary cutting squares, rectangles, and other shapes begins with cutting accurate strips.

1. Press your fabric; then fold it in half with the selvages together. Place the fabric on your cutting mat with the folded edge nearest to your body. Align the Bias Square ruler with the fold of the fabric and place a 6" x 24" ruler to the left so that the raw edges of the fabric are covered.

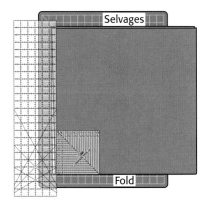

2. Remove the Bias Square ruler and make a rotary cut along the right side of the long ruler. Remove the long ruler and remove the waste strip. This is known as a cleanup cut.

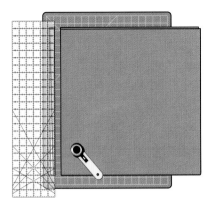

3. To cut strips, align the desired strip width measurement on the ruler with the cut edge of the fabric and carefully cut the strip. After cutting three or four strips, realign the Bias Square ruler along the fold and make a new cleanup cut.

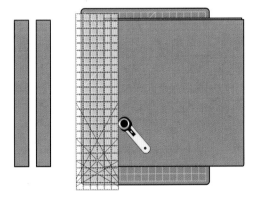

Cutting Squares and Rectangles

To cut squares and rectangles, cut strips in the desired widths. Cut the selvage ends off the strip in the same way that you made the cleanup cut. Align the required measurement on the ruler with the left edge of a strip and cut a square or rectangle. Continue cutting until you have the required number of pieces.

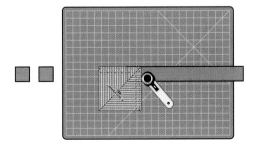

MACHINE PIECING

The most important aspect of machine piecing is sewing a precise ¼" seam allowance. Precision is necessary for the seams to match and the blocks to fit together properly. Some machines have a special presser foot that measures exactly ¼" from the center needle position to the edge of the foot. This allows you to align the edge of your fabric with the edge of the presser foot, resulting in a perfect ¼" seam allowance. On some machines, you can move the needle position to the right or left so that the resulting seam is ¼" from the fabric edge to the stitching line.

If your machine doesn't have either of these features, you can create a seam guide by placing a piece of masking tape ¼" from the needle. Place an accurate ruler or piece of graph paper under the presser foot and lower the needle onto the ¼" seam line. Mark the seam allowance by placing a piece of masking tape at the edge of the ruler or paper. Be careful not to cover the feed dogs on your sewing machine. Use several layers of masking tape, building a raised edge to guide your fabric. You can also use moleskin or a magnetic seam guide.

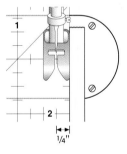

TESTING FOR ACCURACY

To test the accuracy of your ¼" seam, follow these steps:

1. *Cut two pieces of fabric, each 1¼" x 3".*
2. *Sew the rectangles together using the edge of the presser foot or the seam guide you have made. Press the seam allowances to one side. After it is sewn and pressed, the strip should measure exactly 2" wide. If it doesn't, adjust the needle or seam guide and sew another set of strips.*

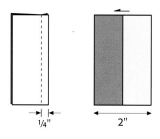

PRESSING

Pressing is one of the keys to precise piecing. Set your iron on the cotton setting. Use a padded pressing surface to prevent the seam allowance from creating a ridge on the right side of the unit. To avoid possible distortion, allow the pieces to cool before moving them from the pressing surface.

After stitching a seam, it is important to carefully press your work. Press seams to one side. When sewing one unit to another, press seams that need to match in opposite directions. The two opposing seams will hold each other in place and evenly distribute the fabric bulk.

Pressing arrows are included in the project illustrations when it is necessary to press the seams in a specific direction. Following the arrows will help in constructing the blocks and assembling the quilt top. When no arrows are indicated, the direction in which

POSITIONING PINS

When triangles are joined to other fabric pieces, the stitching lines cross each other on the back, creating an X at the seam line. Stitch through the center of the X to maintain a crisp point on your triangles. A positioning pin will help you match two points. As shown below, place the triangles right sides together and insert a positioning pin through the wrong side of the first triangle, right at the tip. Then pull the two triangle points far enough apart to see the tip of the second triangle. Push the pin straight through the second triangle tip to establish the matching point. Note that you do not lock the positioning pin into the fabric; it should remain loose. Then lock a pin into the fabric on each sides of the positioning pin. Pin the remainder of the seam normally and remove the positioning pin before stitching.

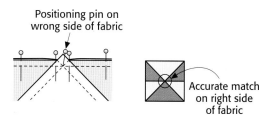

Positioning pin on wrong side of fabric

Accurate match on right side of fabric

you press the seam is your choice. In general, press seams toward the darker fabric or toward the section with fewer seams unless instructed otherwise.

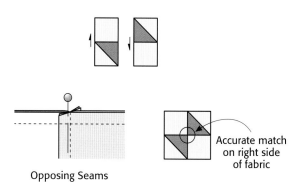

Opposing Seams

Accurate match on right side of fabric

SEW-AND-TRIM TECHNIQUES

Most of the basket blocks use more than one sew-and-trim technique. Sew-and-trim techniques make use of strips, rectangles, and squares that are sewn together and trimmed to make units for the blocks. Along with the directions for each quilt is a handy box listing the sew-and-trim techniques used and their page numbers. Refer to those pages whenever you need additional details about a technique.

Many of the quilts in this book include half-square-triangle units—two half-square triangles sewn together to make a square. I use two different methods for making half-square-triangle units. Both are quick and accurate. The method I choose depends on the number and size of half-square-triangle units I need for the entire project; one is best for making several units at once, each smaller than 3", and the other is best for making individual units 3" or larger.

Multiple Half-Square-Triangle Units

This method is one of the easiest and most accurate ways to make several half-square-triangle units at a time. Bias strips are sewn together to make a strip set. The strip set is cut into squares to make the half-square-triangle units. The units do not become distorted because the sewing and pressing are done before the units are cut. The following instructions begin with two 8" squares of fabric that will yield eight 2½" half-square-triangle units. The size of the fabric square and the width of the bias strips are specified in the cutting directions for each quilt. For any size square, cut bias strips in the required width across the entire square. This method works best for half-square-triangle units that finish less than 3" x 3".

1. Layer two 8" squares with right sides facing up; cut in half diagonally.

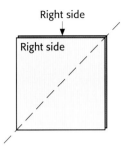

2. Using the first cut as a guide, cut bias strips in the required width for the quilt you are making.

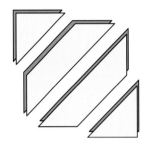

3. Separate and rearrange the strips, alternating the colors. You will have two sets of strips.

4. Sew the strips together along the bias edges, offsetting the point at the top edge ¼" as shown. Carefully press all seams toward the dark fabric. For the best results, press after sewing each seam.

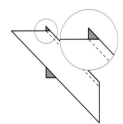 

5. Position a Bias Square ruler with the 45° angle on a seam line. Align the longer cutting ruler with the edge of the Bias Square ruler so that the uneven ends of the strip are covered. Remove the Bias Square ruler and trim the edge of the unit.

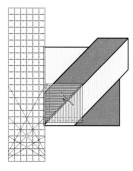

Place the 45° line of a Bias Square ruler along a seam to accurately position the cutting ruler.

6. Cut a segment from the strip set in the required width for the quilt you are making. Continue cutting segments, realigning the 45° diagonal line if needed. Maintaining a true 45° angle is critical to producing accurate units.

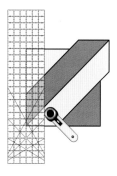

7. Using one cut segment, place a Bias Square ruler so that the edge of the ruler is even with the bottom edge of the fabric, and the 45° diagonal line is along a seam line. Cut on the right side of the ruler. Continue cutting the segments, positioning the diagonal line of the ruler on each seam line.

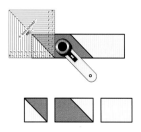

8. Turn the cut segments (or mat) around so the right-hand cuts are now to your left. Working on one segment at a time, position the Bias Square ruler so that the edge of the ruler is even with the bottom edge of the fabric and the 45° diagonal line is along the seam line. Cut on the right side of the ruler to complete one half-square-triangle unit. Repeat with all the segments.

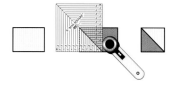

HELPFUL TIP

If you have extra fabric after cutting the half-square-triangle units, continue to cut smaller half-square-triangle units for use in a later project. The extra, smaller-sized units will accumulate quickly, ready to use in another scrappy quilt.

Half-Square-Triangle Units

When you want a scrappy look or need finished half-square-triangle units that are 3" or larger, this method works well. In this method, pressing the unit is the final step, so take extra care not to distort the half-square-triangle unit while pressing.

1. Cut the squares the size specified in the cutting list. (This measurement equals the finished short side of the triangle + ⅞".)

2. With a sharp pencil and ruler, draw a diagonal line from corner to corner on the wrong side of the lighter fabric. Layer two squares right sides together with the marked square on top and raw edges aligned. Sew ¼" on each side of the drawn diagonal line.

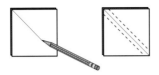

3. Cut on the drawn line with a rotary cutter and ruler. Press the seams toward the darker fabric unless instructed otherwise. Trim the dog-ears, the little triangles that stick out at the corners. Each pair of squares will yield two half-square-triangle units.

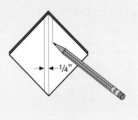
MAKING UNITS FROM STRIP SETS

You can make multiple units more accurately and efficiently if you sew strips into strip sets and then cross-cut them into segments. By cutting with a rotary cutter, you can cut many pieces at the same time. The following steps describe how to make strip sets for a four-patch unit; use the same process for constructing other strip sets and units.

1. Cut the specified number of strips in the required width for the quilt you are making. Arrange the strips in the correct color combinations. With right sides together, sew the strips together along the long edges. Press the seams toward the darker fabric.

2. Place one strip set on top of the other strip set, right sides together, with the light fabric on top of the dark fabric.

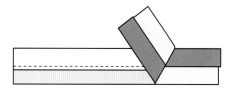

3. Trim the ends of the strip sets and cut the strip sets into segments. The width of each segment is specified in the directions for the quilt you are making.

4. Stitch the segment pairs together using a ¼" seam allowance.

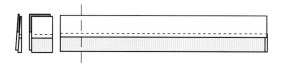

Four-Patch Unit

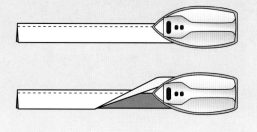
Making Flying-Geese Units

Many of the blocks in this book contain flying-geese units. The following steps describe a quick and easy method for making these units using squares and rectangles. This method eliminates cutting triangles and is very accurate.

1. Using a sharp pencil and ruler, draw a diagonal line from corner to corner on the wrong side of two squares.

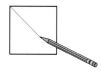

2. Place a marked square on one end of a rectangle, right sides together and raw edges aligned. Stitch directly on the marked line. Trim away the excess fabric, leaving a ¼" seam allowance. Press the seam toward the square.

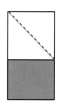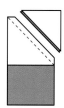

3. Place the second marked square on the other end of the rectangle, right sides together and raw edges aligned. Stitch directly on the marked line. Trim away the excess fabric, leaving a ¼" seam allowance. Press the seam toward the square.

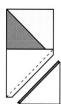

Flying-Geese Unit

MAKING BLOCKS

The instructions and diagrams for each quilt project show the order in which to sew the pieces to make the blocks. In most cases, the shortest seams will be sewn first to make a unit. Many of the basket blocks have units that are sewn first and then trimmed. In general, there are two trimming techniques. The first technique is used for units that are trimmed ¼" beyond crossed seams on the diagonal. The second technique is used for units that are trimmed to make a half-square triangle (a triangle with one 90° angle and two 45° angles).

Trimming Units with Crossed Seams

This sew-and-trim technique is used in almost all of the blocks as the next to the last step before completing the block. It is also used to make units in some of the blocks, as in "Cranberry Baskets" (page 59), "Spring Baskets" (page 54), and "Grandma's Baskets" (page 70). When trimming the units, take care to include an accurate ¼" seam allowance to avoid cutting off a point when stitching the next piece or unit.

After making the unit, align your ruler so that the 45° diagonal line is along the seam line and the ¼" mark is on the crossed seams of the unit. Trim the excess fabric ¼" from the crossed seams.

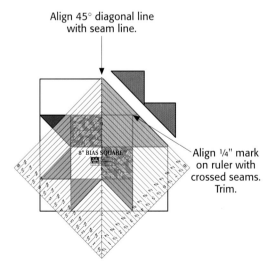

Align 45° diagonal line with seam line.

Align ¼" mark on ruler with crossed seams. Trim.

Trimming Units to Make a Triangle

This sew-and-trim method eliminates the need for templates when making the angled units in blocks for quilts such as "Baskets of Roses" (page 75) and "Baskets of Chicks" (page 85).

After making the unit of squares and rectangles as directed, align your ruler so that the 45° diagonal line is along the outside edge of the unit and the edge of the ruler is on the corner of the unit. Trim the excess fabric to make a half-square triangle.

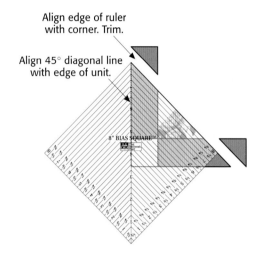

Align edge of ruler with corner. Trim.

Align 45° diagonal line with edge of unit.

Aᴠᴛᴇʀ ᴛʜᴇ blocks are complete, arrange them in either a straight or diagonal setting as directed in the specific project.

STRAIGHT SETTING

1. Arrange the blocks in rows as shown in the quilt assembly diagram for your project, adding the sashing if applicable.

2. Sew the blocks together in horizontal rows. Press the seams in opposite directions from one row to the next unless instructed otherwise. If you have sashing in your quilt, press all of the seams toward the sashing; if you have two different blocks that alternate with each other in your quilt, press all of the seams toward the same block. The pressing arrows in the diagrams indicate which direction to press the seams.

Straight-Set Quilt

3. Pin the rows together, being careful to match the seams from row to row. Sew the rows together and press the seams all in one direction unless instructed otherwise.

HELPFUL TIP

When assembling the quilt top, pieces that are supposed to match may be slightly different sizes. To ease different-sized pieces together, pin the ends, the points that should match, and in between as needed to distribute the excess fabric. Sew with the shortest piece on top, and the feed dogs will ease in the fullness of the bottom piece.

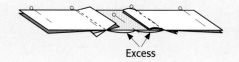

Excess

DIAGONAL SETTING

The blocks for diagonal settings are placed on point and arranged in diagonal rows. Corner and side setting triangles are then added to fill in the corner and side spaces. Side triangles should have the straight of grain along the long outside edge, and corner triangles should have the straight of grain along both short outside edges. Proper placement of the triangles (and grain lines) will prevent sagging and ruffled edges. To ensure that the straight of grain will be placed correctly, cut half-square triangles (squares cut once diagonally) and quarter-square triangles (squares cut twice diagonally) as specified in the directions. These triangles are cut slightly larger than necessary and will be trimmed after the quilt is assembled.

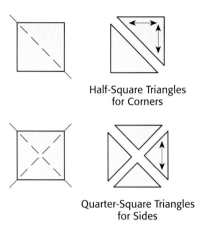

Half-Square Triangles
for Corners

Quarter-Square Triangles
for Sides

1. Arrange the blocks, side triangles, and corner triangles as shown in the quilt assembly diagram for your project, adding sashing if applicable. The setting triangles will be slightly larger than necessary, and they will be trimmed before the borders are added. The cutting directions indicate how large to cut the squares.

2. Sew the blocks and side triangles together in diagonal rows; press the seams in opposite directions from row to row unless instructed otherwise.

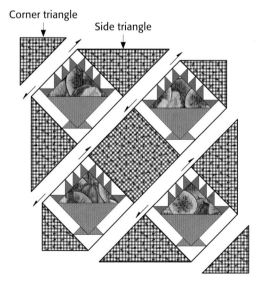

Corner triangle

Side triangle

Diagonally Set Quilt

3. Sew the rows together, matching the seams from row to row. Sew the corner triangles on last.

HELPFUL TIP

When stitching the diagonal rows, align the 90° corner of the side triangles with the blocks. Stitch and press the seam; then trim the excess triangle point even with the edge of the block.

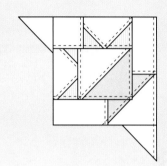

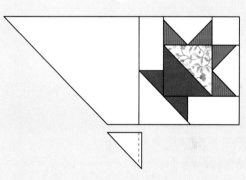

When adding the corner triangles, fold the triangle in half and lightly crease to mark the center of the long side. Fold the block in half and lightly crease to mark the center. Stitch the triangle to the block, matching the center creases; press toward the corner triangle.

Crease

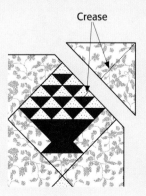

4. To trim the edges of the quilt top, align the ¼" mark on your ruler with the outside corners of the blocks. Using a rotary cutter, trim the excess fabric ¼" from these points, making sure the corners of the quilt are square. Follow the specific trimming instructions for the quilt that you are making.

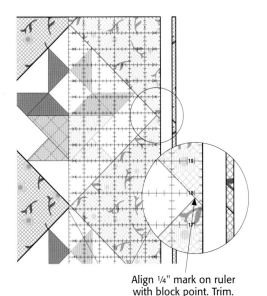

Align ¼" mark on ruler
with block point. Trim.

BORDERS WITH OVERLAPPED CORNERS

The simplest border is a border with overlapped corners. Most of the quilts in this book have this type of border. Borders wider than 2" are cut on the lengthwise grain so they will be stable and will not have to be pieced. You will save fabric if you attach the border to the longer sides first and then attach it to the remaining two sides. Narrow borders (less than 2" wide) are cut across the width of the fabric, unless otherwise noted, and joined together with a diagonal seam to achieve the required length. This is the most fabric-efficient way to cut narrow border strips.

CUTTING TRIANGLES FOR DIAGONAL SETTINGS

Use the handy chart below as a quick and easy reference for cutting squares for side and corner triangles. Use the diagonal block measurement to calculate quilt size, if desired, by simply multiplying the diagonal measurement by the number of blocks.

Finished Block	Diagonal Measurement	Side Triangles	Corner Triangles
6"	8½"	10¼"	5½"
7"	9⅞"	11¾"	6¼"
8"	11⅜"	13"	7"
9"	12¾"	14½"	7⅝"
10"	14⅛"	16"	8⅜"
12"	17"	18¾"	9¾"
14"	19⅞"	21½"	11⅛"
16"	22⅝"	24⅜"	12½"

Measuring for Length of Border Strips

To find the correct measurement for the border strips, always measure through the center of the quilt, not at the outside edges. This ensures that the borders are of equal length on opposite sides of the quilt and helps keep your quilt square.

1. Measure the length of the quilt top through the center. Cut two border strips to this measurement, piecing as necessary.

Measure center of
quilt, top to bottom.

2. Mark the center of the border strips and the quilt top. Pin the borders to the sides of the quilt top, matching centers and ends. Ease or slightly stretch the quilt top to fit the border strips as necessary. Sew the side borders in place and press the seams toward the borders.

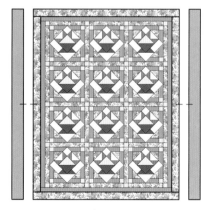

Mark centers.

3. Measure the width of the quilt top through the center, including the side borders, to determine the length of the top and bottom border strips. Cut two border strips to this measurement, piecing as necessary. Mark the center of the border strips and the quilt top. Pin the borders to the top and bottom of the quilt top, matching centers and ends. Ease or slightly stretch the quilt to fit the border strips as necessary.

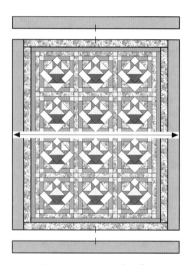

Measure center of quilt,
side to side, including
borders. Mark centers.

4. Sew the top and bottom borders in place and press the seams toward the border strip.

Quilts consist of three layers—the quilt top, backing, and batting. Now that your quilt top is done, you're ready to move on to the finishing stages.

MAKING THE BACKING

Cut a piece of fabric 4" to 6" larger than the quilt top (2" to 3" on all sides). For quilts wider than the width of your fabric, you will need to piece the backing. The seam can run horizontally or vertically unless the fabric is a print that is best viewed from a specific direction. When piecing the backing, be sure to trim off the selvages before sewing the pieces together. Press the seam open to reduce the bulk. For the quilts in this book, all of the yardage amounts for backing fabric allow enough leftover fabric so that you can cut a hanging sleeve to match the backing.

If you don't have enough of any one fabric to make the backing, you can do some creative piecing. I often sew four fabrics together to make a large four-patch; this creates a fun backing with only two seams, and I get to use up fabric in my stash.

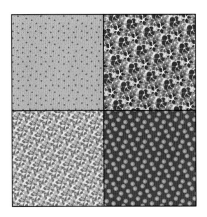

A Four-Patch Backing

PREPARING THE BATTING

There are many types of batting to choose from. The type of batting you choose will depend on whether you plan to hand or machine quilt your quilt top. New battings are always being developed. Check with your favorite quilt shop for the most recent products. Generally, the thinner the batting—whether cotton or polyester—the easier it is to hand quilt. For machine quilting, a cotton batting works best. It won't move or slip between the quilt top and backing.

You can buy batting by the yard or packaged in standard bed sizes. If you are using prepackaged batting, open the package and smooth the batting out flat. Allow the batting to rest in this position for at least 24 hours. The batting should be large enough to allow 2" of extra batting around all edges of the quilt top.

LAYERING THE QUILT

Give the quilt top and backing a careful pressing before you layer the quilt. Then follow the steps below to assemble the quilt layers.

1. Spread the backing, wrong side up, on a flat, clean surface. Anchor it with pins or masking tape. Be careful not to stretch the backing out of shape.

2. Spread the batting over the backing, smoothing out any wrinkles.

3. Place the pressed quilt top, right side up, on top of the batting. Smooth out any wrinkles and make sure the edges of the quilt top are parallel to the edges of the backing. Smooth from the center out and along straight lines to ensure that the blocks and borders remain straight.

4. For hand quilting, baste with needle and thread, starting in the center and working diagonally to each corner. Continue basting in a grid of horizontal and vertical lines 6" to 8" apart. To finish, baste around the edges about ⅛" from the edge of the quilt top. For machine quilting, baste the layers with #2 rustproof safety pins. Place pins 4" to 6" apart; try to avoid areas where you intend to quilt.

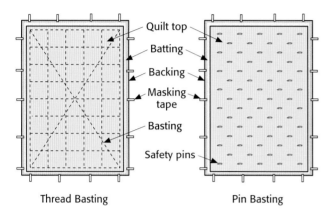

Thread Basting   Pin Basting

QUILTING

To decide how much quilting is needed, use the general rule that any unquilted spaces should be no bigger than 4" x 4". Check the batting that you will be using to see the recommended amount of quilting. The density of quilting should be similar throughout the entire quilt so that the quilt will remain square and not become distorted.

Quilting by Hand

To quilt by hand, you will need short, sturdy needles called Betweens, as well as quilting thread and a thimble to fit the middle finger of your sewing hand. Use the smallest needle you can comfortably handle; the finer the needle, the smaller your stitches will be. Most quilters also use a frame or hoop to support their work.

An excellent book to help you learn all about hand quilting techniques is *Loving Stitches: A Guide to Fine Hand Quilting, Revised Edition*, by Jeana Kimball (Martingale & Company).

Quilting by Machine

All of my quilts are quilted by machine. Machine quilting is suitable for all types and sizes of quilts and allows you to complete a quilt quickly. For straight-line quilting, such as quilting in the ditch, outline quilting, or grids, it is extremely helpful to have a walking foot to help feed the layers through the machine evenly without shifting or puckering. Some machines have a built-in walking foot; other machines require a separate attachment.

Walking Foot Attachment

Quilting in the Ditch   Outline Quilting

For free-motion quilting, you need a darning foot and the ability to drop the feed dogs on your machine. With free-motion quilting, you guide the fabric and determine stitch length by the speed at which you run the machine and feed the fabric under the foot. Use free-motion quilting to outline designs in the fabric or to create stippling and many other designs.

Darning Foot

Stippling   Free-Motion Stars

♦ *Plan a design that has continuous long lines. Complete all of the straight-line quilting with the walking foot, and then switch to the darning foot, lower the feed dog, and start the free-motion quilting.*

♦ *Use a sewing machine needle with a large eye, such as a 90/14, that will not shred the thread.*

♦ *Before you begin quilting, make a sample square consisting of two 6" squares of fabric and a 6" square of batting. Practice controlling the motion of the fabric with your hands and controlling the speed of the machine until you feel comfortable. Look at both sides of the sample to check the thread tension; adjust the tension on your machine if necessary.*

♦ *Start and stop each quilting line by shortening the stitch length for the first and last ⅛" to ¼".*

♦ *For more information on machine quilting, refer to* Machine Quilting Made Easy! *by Maurine Noble (Martingale & Company, 1994).*

SQUARING UP A QUILT

When you complete the quilting, you will need to square up your quilt before sewing on the binding. Align a ruler with the seam line of the outer border and measure the width of the outer border in several places. Use the narrowest measurement for trimming. Position a ruler along the seam line of the outer border and trim the excess batting and backing from all four sides. At each corner, use a large square ruler to square up the corners.

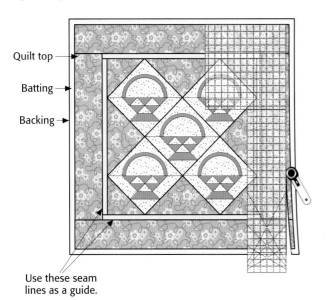

Quilt top

Batting

Backing

Use these seam lines as a guide.

BINDING

The binding is a wonderful opportunity to add to the overall look of your quilt. If you want the binding to frame the outer border or act as an additional border, use a fabric that is different from the outer border, as I did in "Picnic Baskets" on page 80. If you prefer that the binding "disappear," use the same fabric for the binding as for the outer border.

I prefer a double-fold binding made from straight-grain strips. Straight-grain binding is easier to work with and takes less fabric that bias-cut binding. I cut strips 2" wide for a narrow finished binding. Depending on your batting choice and your preference, you may want to cut wider strips. You will need enough strips to go around the perimeter of the quilt plus about 10" for making seams and turning corners. The number of strips is specified in the cutting directions for each quilt.

If you are going to attach a sleeve to the back of your quilt for hanging, refer to "Adding a Sleeve" on page 22 and attach it now, before you bind the edges.

1. Cut 2"-wide strips across the width of the fabric as required for your quilt.

2. Make one long continuous strip by sewing the strips at right angles and stitching on the diagonal as shown. Trim the excess fabric, leaving a ¼" seam allowance, and press the seams open.

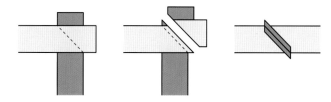

3. Fold the binding in half lengthwise, with the wrong sides together, and press. Unfold the binding at one end; trim and turn under ¼" at a 45° angle as shown.

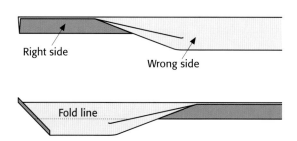

4. Starting on the bottom edge of the quilt, stitch the binding to the quilt using a ¼" seam allowance. Begin stitching 3" from the start of the binding. Stop stitching ¼" from the first corner and backstitch.

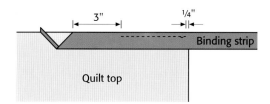

5. Remove the quilt from the sewing machine. Fold the binding away from the quilt, and then fold again as shown, to create an angled pleat at the corner.

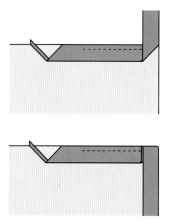

6. Start stitching at the fold of the binding. Backstitch at the beginning of the seam and then continue stitching along the edge of the quilt top. Stop ¼" from the corner and backstitch. Repeat step 5 to form the mitered corner. Continue stitching around the quilt, repeating the mitering process at each corner.

7. When you reach the beginning of the binding, stop 3" before the starting end and backstitch. Remove the quilt from the machine. Trim the end 1" longer than needed and tuck the end inside the beginning strip. Pin in place, making sure the strip lies flat. Stitch the rest of the binding.

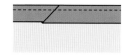

8. Turn the binding to the back of the quilt. Hand stitch the binding in place with the folded edge covering the row of machine stitching. Use thread that matches the binding. At each corner, fold the binding to form a miter on the back of the quilt.

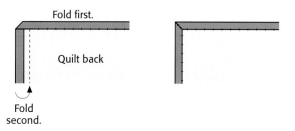

ADDING A SLEEVE

If you plan to hang your quilt, attach a sleeve or rod pocket to the back before attaching the binding. From the leftover backing fabric, cut an 8"-wide strip of fabric equal to the width of your quilt. You may need to piece two or three strips together for larger quilts.

1. On each end of the strip, fold over ½", and then fold ½" again. Press and stitch by machine.

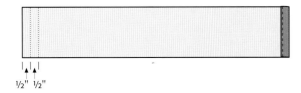

½" ½"

2. Fold the strip in half lengthwise, wrong sides together; baste the raw edges to the top edge of the back of your quilt. These will be secured when you sew on the binding. Your quilt should be about 1" wider than the sleeve on both sides.

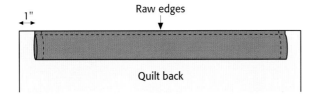

Raw edges

1"

Quilt back

3. Make a small pleat in the sleeve to accommodate the thickness of the rod, and then slip-stitch the ends and bottom edge of the sleeve to the backing fabric. This keeps the rod from being inserted next to the quilt backing.

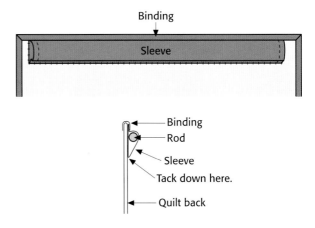

Binding

Sleeve

Binding
Rod
Sleeve
Tack down here.
Quilt back

ADDING A LABEL

A label provides important information including the name of the quilt, the person who made it, when it was made, and where it was made. You may also want to include the name of the recipient if the quilt is a gift, and any other interesting or important information. A label can be as elaborate or as simple as you desire.

To make a label, press a piece of freezer paper to the wrong side of a piece of muslin or light-colored fabric to stabilize it while you write. Use a permanent-ink fabric pen to write all of the information. To help you write straight, draw lines on the freezer paper with a marker to use as a guide. You should be able to see the lines through the fabric.

When the label is complete, remove the freezer paper. Fold and press the raw edges to the wrong side of the label. Stitch the label to the back of the quilt with a blind hem stitch.

Pieced by Nancy Mahoney and Quilted by Gretchen Engel · Finished Quilt: 64½" x 64½" · Finished Block: 10"

I love the freshness of red, white, and blue; it never goes out of style. The sawtooth border makes this wonderful traditional quilt particularly dramatic. A variety of blue prints were used in the baskets to create a scrappy look, and the cream prints for the background provide a nice contrast for the bold reds and blues.

MATERIALS

All yardages are based on 42"-wide fabric.

- 2⅛ yards of navy print for blocks, border, and binding
- 1⅞ yards of cream print A for blocks and sashing
- ⅞ yard of blue print A for blocks and setting triangles
- ¾ yard of blue print B for blocks and sawtooth border
- ¾ yard of cream print B for blocks and sawtooth border
- ⅝ yard of red print B for blocks and sashing squares
- ½ yard of red print A for blocks and inner border
- 1 fat eighth *each* of 6 blue prints for blocks
- 1 fat eighth *each* of 7 cream prints for blocks
- 4¼ yards of fabric for backing
- 68" x 68" piece of batting

SEW-AND-TRIM TECHNIQUES
⌢

Multiple Half-Square-Triangle Units (page 9)
Half-Square-Triangle Units (page 10)
Making Flying-Geese Units (page 12)
Trimming Units with Crossed Seams (page 13)

CUTTING

From blue print A, cut:

- 2 squares, 17⅜" x 17⅜"; cut twice diagonally to yield 8 triangles
- 2 squares, 9¾" x 9¾"; cut once diagonally to yield 4 triangles
- 1 square, 7" x 7"

From *each* of the 6 blue print fat eighths, cut:

- 1 square, 7" x 7" (6 total)

From *each* of the 7 cream print fat eighths, cut:

- 1 square, 7" x 7" (7 total)

From red print B, cut:

- 2 squares, 9" x 9"
- 52 squares, 2½" x 2½"
- 12 squares, 1½" x 1½"

From cream print A, cut:

- 2 squares, 9" x 9"
- 12 strips, 1½" x 42"; crosscut into 12 rectangles, 1½" x 11½", and 24 rectangles, 1½" x 10½"
- 10 strips, 2½" x 42"; crosscut into 26 rectangles, 2½" x 6½"; 26 rectangles, 2½" x 4½"; and 13 squares, 2½" x 2½"
- 7 squares, 4⅞" x 4⅞"; cut once diagonally to yield 13 triangles (14 total; 1 is extra)

From blue print B, cut:

- 8 squares, 10" x 10"

From cream print B, cut:

- 8 squares, 10" x 10"

From red print A, cut:

- 5 strips, 1½" x 42"
- 7 squares, 4⅞" x 4⅞"

From the navy print, cut:

- 4 strips, 5½" x the lengthwise grain
- 4 binding strips, 2" x the lengthwise grain
- 7 squares, 4⅞" x 4⅞"
- 26 squares, 2½" x 2½"

MAKING THE BLOCKS

1. Pair each 7" blue square with each cream 7" square, right sides facing up. Cut and piece 2½"-wide bias strips. Make 14 strip sets. Cut 56 half-square-triangle units, each 2½" x 2½".

Make 14 strip sets.
Cut 56 units.

2. Pair each 9" red print B square with each 9" cream print A square, right sides facing up. Cut and piece 2½"-wide bias strips. Make 4 strip sets. Cut 26 half-square-triangle units, each 2½" x 2½".

Make 4 strip sets.
Cut 26 units.

3. Pair each 10" blue print B square with each 10" cream print B square, right sides facing up. Cut and piece 2½"-wide bias strips. Make 16 strip sets. Cut 9 half-square-triangle units for the blocks and 104 half-square-triangle units for the sawtooth border, each 2½" x 2½".

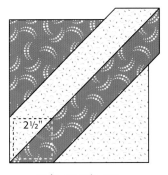

Make 16 strip sets.
Cut 113 units.

4. Draw a diagonal line from corner to corner on the wrong side of each red 4⅞" square. Place a marked red square on a navy 4⅞" square, right sides together; stitch ¼" on each side of the drawn diagonal line. Cut and press. Make 13 half-square-triangle units, each 4½" x 4½". (You will have 14 total; 1 is extra.)

Make 13.

5. Sew two 2½" red print B squares and one 2½" x 4½" cream print A rectangle together to make a flying-geese unit; press. Make 26.

Make 26.

6. Sew a navy 2½" square to one end of a 2½" x 6½" cream print A rectangle to make a side unit. Press toward the navy square. Make 26.

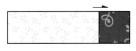

Make 26.

7. Sew five half-square-triangle units from steps 1 and 3 and one half-square-triangle unit from step 4 into rows as shown; press. Sew the rows together and press. Make 13.

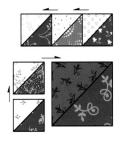 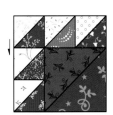

Make 13.

8. Sew two flying-geese units from step 5, two half-square-triangle units from step 2, one 2½" cream print A square, and the unit from step 7 into rows as shown; press. Sew the rows together; press. Make 13.

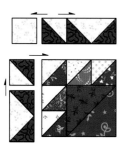

Make 13.

DESIGN OPTION

Here's an option that will give you a completely different look. Set four blocks side by side in a straight setting. Add a wide floral stripe for the border.

BASKETS IN THE MEADOW
Pieced by Nancy Mahoney and Quilted by Barbara Ford

9. Sew two side units from step 6 and the unit from step 8 together as shown; press. Trim the navy squares, leaving a ¼" seam allowance beyond the crossed seams. Make 13.

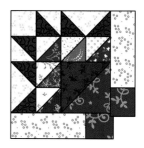
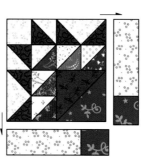

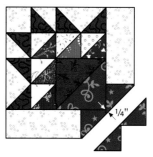

Make 13.

10. Fold a cream print A triangle in half and lightly press to mark the center of the long side. Sew a cream triangle to the unit from step 9, matching the center crease and the crossed seam to complete one block. Press toward the cream triangle. Make 13 blocks.

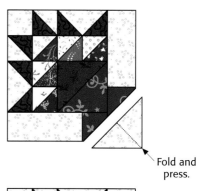

Fold and press.

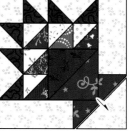

Make 13.

QUILT TOP ASSEMBLY

1. Referring to "Assembling the Quilt Top" on pages 14–17, lay out the basket blocks, sashing strips, and sashing squares in diagonal rows. Add the blue 17⅜" side triangles.

2. Sew the blocks, sashing strips, and side triangles together in rows, pressing toward the sashing strips.

3. Sew the sashing strips and sashing squares together in rows, pressing toward the sashing strips.

4. Sew the block rows and sashing rows together, pressing toward the sashing rows.

5. Add the 9¾" corner triangles last and press toward the triangles.

6. Square up the quilt top, trimming the edges ¼" from the corners of the blocks as needed. The quilt top should measure 48½" x 48½".

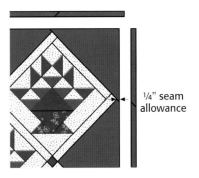

¼" seam allowance

ADDING THE BORDERS

For detailed instructions, refer to "Borders with Overlapped Corners" on pages 16–17.

1. Join the red 1½" x 42" strips end to end to make one continuous strip. Measure and cut two border strips to 1½" x 48½".

2. Sew the trimmed red inner-border strips to the side edges of the quilt top. Press toward the border strips.

3. Measure the quilt through the center from side to side, including the border just added. It should measure 50½" wide. Cut two border strips to that measurement.

4. Sew the trimmed red inner-border strips to the top and bottom edges of the quilt top. Press toward the border strips. The quilt top should measure 50½" x 50½" for the sawtooth border to fit.

5. Sew 25 half-square-triangle units, from step 3 in "Making the Blocks," together in rows; press. Make four sawtooth rows.

Make 4.

6. Sew sawtooth rows to the side edges of the quilt top. Press toward the red border.

7. Sew one half-square-triangle unit to each end of the remaining two sawtooth rows. Press the seam allowance toward the half-square-triangle unit. Sew the sawtooth rows to the top and bottom edges of the quilt top. Press toward the red border.

8. Measure the quilt through the center as you did before to add the navy outer-border strips. Press toward the outer border.

FINISHING THE QUILT

For detailed instructions on finishing techniques, refer to "Finishing" on pages 18–22.

1. Cut and piece the backing fabric so it is 4" to 6" larger than the quilt top. Layer the quilt top with batting and backing. Baste the layers together.

2. Hand or machine quilt as desired.

3. Square up the quilt sandwich.

4. Using the navy 2" strips, prepare and sew the binding to the quilt. Add a hanging sleeve, if desired, and a label.

Quilting suggestions: Quilt a medallion in the large half-square-triangle unit of each basket; quilt in the ditch around the remainder of the basket blocks. Quilt a partial medallion in the side and corner triangles. Quilt a continuous design in the navy border.

Pieced and Quilted by Nancy Mahoney · Finished Quilt: 52" x 52" · Finished Block: 8"

These charming baskets are very easy and quick to make using mainly squares and rectangles. The four-patch border softens the edges and adds visual interest—without adding extra difficulty. Five fabrics are all it takes to make this lovely quilt.

MATERIALS

All yardages are based on 42"-wide fabric.

♦ 2⅛ yards of cream print for block backgrounds, pieced border, setting blocks, and setting triangles

♦ 1⅝ yards of large-scale black floral print for borders

♦ ⅝ yard of red print for blocks and pieced border

♦ ⅝ yard of green print for blocks and binding

♦ ¼ yard of black print for blocks

♦ 3½ yards of fabric for backing

♦ 56" x 56" piece of batting

CUTTING

From the cream print, cut:

♦ 4 squares, 8½" x 8½"

♦ 2 squares, 13" x 13"; cut twice diagonally to yield 8 triangles

♦ 2 squares, 7" x 7"; cut once diagonally to yield 4 triangles

♦ 4 strips, 2" x 42"

♦ 1 strip, 2½" x 42"; crosscut into 9 squares, 2½" x 2½"

♦ 5 strips, 2½" x 42"; crosscut into 36 rectangles, 2½" x 4½"

♦ 1 strip, 2½" x 24"

♦ 5 squares, 4⅞" x 4⅞"; cut once diagonally to yield 9 triangles (10 total; 1 is extra)

♦ 8 squares, 5½" x 5½"; cut twice diagonally to yield 32 triangles

♦ 2 squares, 3" x 3"; cut once diagonally to yield 4 triangles

From the black print, cut:

♦ 2 strips, 2½" x 42"; crosscut into 2 strips, 2½" x 24"

From the green print, cut:

♦ 6 binding strips, 2" x 42"

♦ 2 strips, 2½" x 42"; crosscut into 18 squares, 2½" x 2½", and 1 strip, 2½" x 24"

From the red print, cut:

♦ 4 strips, 2" x 42"

♦ 3 strips, 2½" x 42"; crosscut into 36 squares, 2½" x 2½"

♦ 1 rectangle, 2" x 15"

From the large-scale black floral print, cut:

♦ 4 strips, 5" x the lengthwise grain

♦ 1 rectangle, 2" x 15"

♦ 8 squares, 5½" x 5½"; cut twice diagonally to yield 32 triangles

♦ 6 squares, 3" x 3"; cut once diagonally to yield 12 triangles

SEW-AND-TRIM TECHNIQUES

Making Units from Strip Sets (page 11)
Making Flying-Geese Units (page 12)
Trimming Units with Crossed Seams (page 13)

MAKING THE BLOCKS

1. Sew the cream 2½" x 24" strip and one black 2½" x 24" strip together to make strip set A. Press toward the black strip. Cut nine segments, 2½" wide.

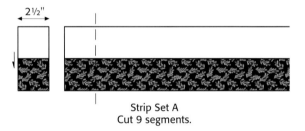

Strip Set A
Cut 9 segments.

2. Sew the green 2½" x 24" strip and the remaining black 2½" x 24" strip together to make strip set B. Press toward the black strip. Cut nine segments, 2½" wide.

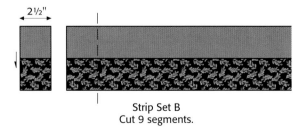

Strip Set B
Cut 9 segments.

3. Sew one segment from strip set A and one segment from strip set B together to make a four-patch unit; press. Make nine four-patch units.

Make 9.

4. Sew two red 2½" squares and one cream 2½" x 4½" rectangle together to make a flying-geese unit; press. Make 18 units.

Make 18.

5. Sew a green 2½" square to one end of a cream 2½" x 4½" rectangle to make a side unit. Press toward the green square. Make 18 side units.

Make 18.

6. Sew one 2½" cream square, one four-patch unit from step 3, and two flying-geese units from step 4 together as shown; press. Make nine.

Make 9.

7. Sew two side units from step 5 and the unit from step 6 together as shown; press. Trim the green squares, leaving a ¼" seam allowance beyond the crossed seams. Make nine.

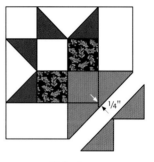

¼"

Make 9.

8. Fold a cream 4⅞" triangle in half and lightly press to mark the center of the long side. Sew the triangle to the unit from step 7, matching the center crease and the crossed seam to complete one block. Press toward the cream triangle. Make nine blocks.

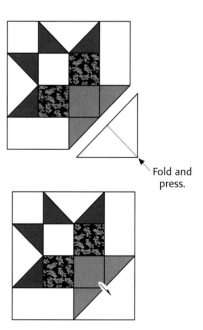

Fold and press.

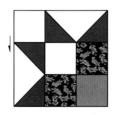

Make 9.

QUILT TOP ASSEMBLY

1. Referring to "Assembling the Quilt Top" on pages 14–17, lay out the basket blocks and 8½" setting squares in diagonal rows. Add the cream 13" side triangles.

2. Sew the blocks, setting squares, and side triangles together in rows, pressing toward the cream print.

3. Sew the rows together, adding the 7" corner triangles last. Press the seams toward the cream print.

4. Square up the quilt top, trimming the edges ¼" from the corners of the blocks as needed. The quilt top should measure 34½" x 34½".

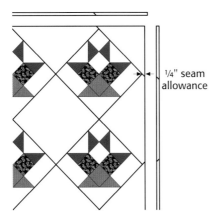

¼" seam allowance

ADDING THE BORDERS

1. Sew one cream 2" x 42" strip and one red 2" x 42" strip together to a make a strip set. Press toward the red strip. Make 4 strip sets. Cut 64 segments, 2" wide.

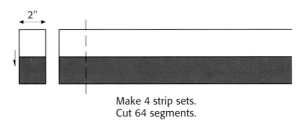

2"

Make 4 strip sets.
Cut 64 segments.

2. Sew two segments into a four-patch unit. Press the seams. Make 32 units.

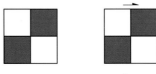

Make 32.

3. Sew the red 2" x 15" rectangle to the black floral 2" x 15" rectangle. Press toward the black floral print. Cut four 3½" corner units.

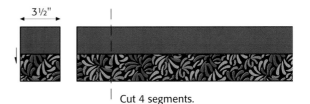

3½"

Cut 4 segments.

4. Sew eight four-patch units from step 2, seven cream 5½" triangles, seven black floral 5½" triangles, two cream 3" triangles, and two black floral 3" triangles together as shown to make a side border strip. Press as indicated. Make two side border strips.

Make 2.

5. Sew eight four-patch units from step 2, two corner units from step 3, nine cream 5½" triangles, nine black floral 5½" triangles, and four black floral 3" triangles together as shown to make a top border strip. Press as shown. Repeat to make the bottom border strip.

Make 2.

6. Sew the side four-patch border strips to the edges of the quilt top. Press toward the center.

7. Sew the remaining four-patch border strips to the top and bottom edges of the quilt top. Press toward the center.

8. Measure the quilt through the center from top to bottom and cut two black floral outer-border strips to fit that measurement. Refer to "Borders with Overlapped Corners" on pages 16–17 for details as needed.

9. Sew the trimmed border strips to the side edges of the quilt top. Press toward the border strips.

10. Measure the quilt through the center from side to side, including the borders just added. Cut two outer-border strips to fit that measurement.

11. Sew the trimmed outer-border strips to the top and bottom edges of the quilt top; press.

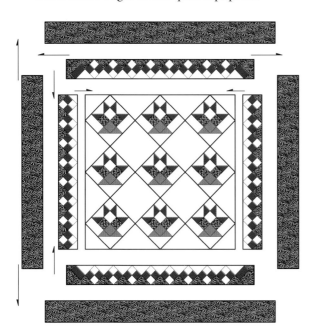

FINISHING THE QUILT

For detailed instructions on finishing techniques, refer to "Finishing" on pages 18–22.

1. Cut and piece the backing fabric so it is 4" to 6" larger than the quilt top. Layer the quilt top with batting and backing. Baste the layers together.

2. Hand or machine quilt as desired.

3. Square up the quilt sandwich.

4. Using the green 2" strips, prepare and sew the binding to the quilt. Add a hanging sleeve, if desired, and a label.

Quilting suggestions: Quilt a medallion over the four-patch unit in each Basket block; quilt the remainder of the block in the ditch. Quilt a medallion in the background squares and a partial medallion in the side triangles. Quilt the pieced border in the ditch and a continuous design in the outer border.

Pieced by Nancy Mahoney and Quilted by Gretchen Engel · Finished Quilt: 58½" x 58½" · Finished Block: 12"

Timeless nine-patch blocks and dark plum sashing create the perfect setting for these unique basket blocks. With this design, the basket block doesn't need to be set on point for the basket to appear vertical. I particularly like how the baskets appear to float on the background. The black print border adds a look of distinction to this marvelous quilt.

MATERIALS

All yardages are based on 42"-wide fabric.

- 2⅜ yards of cream print for block backgrounds and sashing
- 2 yards of black-and-purple floral print for outer border and binding
- 1⅛ yards of purple print for blocks and sashing
- ½ yard of green print for blocks
- ⅜ yard of large-scale floral print for blocks
- 3⅞ yards of fabric for backing
- 63" x 63" piece of batting

CUTTING

From the purple print, cut:
- 13 strips, 1½" x 42"
- 8 squares, 8" x 8"

From the cream print, cut:
- 20 strips, 1½" x 42"
- 4 strips, 6⅞" x 42"; crosscut into 18 squares, 6⅞" x 6⅞"; cut 9 squares once diagonally to yield 18 triangles
- 8 squares, 8" x 8"

From the green print, cut:
- 1 strip, 7¼" x 42"; crosscut into 5 squares, 7¼" x 7¼"
- 1 strip, 3⅞" x 42"; crosscut into 9 squares, 3⅞" x 3⅞"

From the large-scale floral print, cut:
- 1 strip, 7¼" x 42"; crosscut into 5 squares, 7¼" x 7¼"

From the black-and-purple floral, cut:
- 4 strips, 5½" x the lengthwise grain
- 4 binding strips, 2" x the lengthwise grain

SEW-AND-TRIM TECHNIQUES

Multiple Half-Square-Triangle Units (page 9)
Half-Square-Triangle Units (page 10)
Making Units from Strip Sets (page 11)

MAKING THE BLOCKS

1. Pair each purple 8" square with each cream 8" square, right sides facing up. Cut and piece 2¾"-wide bias strips. Make 16 strip sets. Cut 63 half-square-triangle units, each 2⅝" x 2⅝".

Make 16 strip sets.
Cut 63 units.

2. Draw a diagonal line from corner to corner on the wrong side of each green 7¼" square. Place a marked green square on a large-scale floral 7¼" square, right sides together; stitch ¼" on each side of the drawn diagonal line. Cut and press. Make nine half-square-triangle units, each 6⅞" x 6⅞". (You will have 10 total; 1 is extra.)

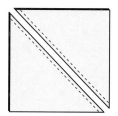

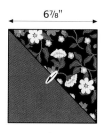

6⅞"

Make 9.

3. Draw a diagonal line from corner to corner on the wrong side of each green 3⅞" square. Place a marked green square on the corner of a cream 6⅞" square as shown, with right sides together and raw edges aligned. Stitch directly on the drawn diagonal line. Trim the corner, leaving a ¼" seam allowance. Press toward the green print. Make nine. Using a ruler and rotary cutter, cut each square on the diagonal to yield nine triangle units and nine reversed triangle units.

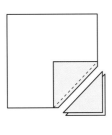

Make 9.

4. Sew seven half-square-triangle units from step 1 and one half-square-triangle unit from step 2 together as shown; press. Make nine.

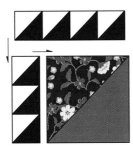

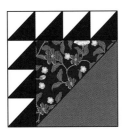

Make 9.

5. Fold the unit from step 4 in half vertically and horizontally, and lightly crease to mark the center of each side. Fold a triangle unit from step 3 and a cream 6⅞" triangle in half and lightly press to mark the center of both long sides. Sew the triangle and triangle unit to opposite sides of the unit from step 4 as shown, matching the center creases; press. Fold and sew a reversed triangle unit from step 3 and a cream 6⅞" triangle to the remaining sides of the unit to complete the block; press. Make nine blocks.

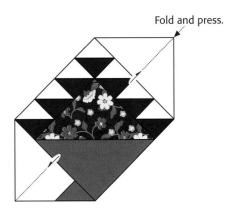

Fold and press.

Make 9.

PIECING THE SASHING

1. Sew two cream 1½" x 42" strips and one purple 1½" x 42" strip together to make strip set A. Press toward the purple strip. Make nine strip sets. Cut 24 segments 12½" wide, and 16 segments 1½" wide.

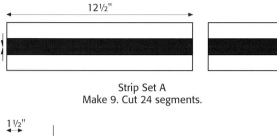

Strip Set A
Make 9. Cut 24 segments.

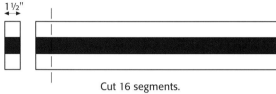

Cut 16 segments.

2. Sew two purple 1½" x 42" strips and one cream 1½" x 42" strip together to make strip set B. Press toward the purple strip. Make two strip sets. Cut 32 segments 1½" wide.

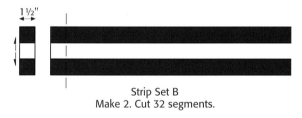

Strip Set B
Make 2. Cut 32 segments.

3. Sew one segment from step 1 and two segments from step 2 together to make a nine-patch unit. Press as shown. Make 16 units.

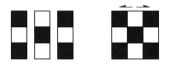

QUILT TOP ASSEMBLY

1. Referring to "Assembling the Quilt Top" on pages 14–17, arrange the blocks in rows, adding the sashing units. Sew four sashing units and three blocks together to make a block row. Press the seams toward the sashing units. Make three rows.

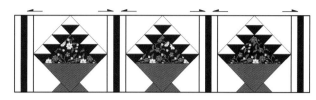

Make 3.

2. Sew four nine-patch units and three sashing units together to make a sashing row. Press the seams toward the sashing units. Make four rows.

Make 4.

3. Sew the block rows and sashing rows together. Press the seams toward the sashing rows.

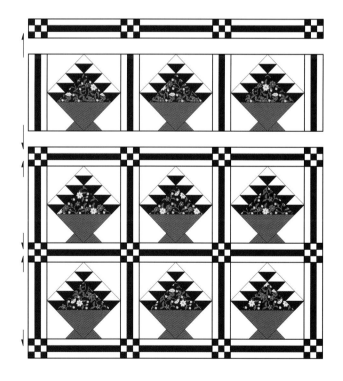

Adding the Borders

For detailed instructions, refer to "Borders with Overlapped Corners" on pages 16–17.

1. Measure the quilt through the center from top to bottom and cut two black-and-purple floral 5½" outer-border strips to fit that measurement.

2. Sew the outer-border strips to the side edges of the quilt top. Press toward the border strips.

3. Measure the quilt through the center from side to side, including the borders just added. Cut two black-and-purple floral 5½" outer-border strips to fit that measurement.

4. Sew the outer-border strips to the top and bottom edges of the quilt top; press.

Finishing the Quilt

For detailed instructions on finishing techniques, refer to "Finishing" on pages 18–22.

1. Cut and piece the backing fabric so it is 4" to 6" larger than the quilt top. Layer the quilt top with batting and backing. Baste the layers together.

2. Hand or machine quilt as desired.

3. Square up the quilt sandwich.

4. Using the black-and-purple floral 2" strips, prepare and sew the binding to the quilt. Add a hanging sleeve, if desired, and a label.

Quilting suggestions: Quilt around each basket in the ditch. Quilt a medallion pattern in the center of the blocks, and a partial medallion in the corner triangles. Quilt the sashing in the ditch and a continuous design in the border.

Pieced and Quilted by Nancy Mahoney · Finished Quilt: 57¾" x 71½" · Finished Block: 11¼"

This striking quilt is made from one of my favorite color combinations: red and yellow. The cheery basket blocks are quick and easy to make. The narrow red sashing and floral border complete the look, adding a little extra pizzazz!

MATERIALS

All yardages are based on 42"-wide fabric.

- 2 yards of large-scale floral print for middle border
- 1¼ yards of cream print for sashing
- 1 yard of red print for outer border, corner-stones, and blocks
- ⅞ yard of yellow-and-red print for blocks
- ⅞ yard of red stripe for sashing and binding
- ¾ yard of ivory print for blocks
- ⅝ yard of gold print for inner border and blocks
- ¼ yard of floral print for blocks
- 3⅞ yards of fabric for backing
- 62" x 76" piece of batting

CUTTING

From the red print, cut:
- 7 strips, 2" x 42"
- 2 strips, 3" x 42"; crosscut into 20 squares, 3" x 3"
- 3 strips, 2½" x 42"; crosscut into 48 squares, 2½" x 2½"

From the ivory print, cut:
- 7 strips, 2½" x 42"; crosscut into 48 rectangles, 2½" x 4½", and 12 squares, 2½" x 2½"
- 1 strip, 4⅞" x 42"; crosscut into 6 squares, 4⅞" x 4⅞"; cut each square once diagonally to yield 12 triangles

From the floral print, cut:
- 1 strip, 4⅞" x 42"; crosscut into 6 squares, 4⅞" x 4⅞"

From the gold print, cut:
- 6 strips, 1¼" x 42"
- 1 strip, 4⅞" x 42"; crosscut into 6 squares, 4⅞" x 4⅞"
- 2 strips, 2½" x 42"; crosscut into 24 squares, 2½" x 2½"

From the yellow-and-red print, cut:
- 4 strips, 6½" x 42"; crosscut into 24 squares, 6½" x 6½"; cut each square once diagonally to yield 48 triangles

From the cream print, cut:
- 26 strips, 1½" x 42"; crosscut 4 strips into 80 squares, 1½" x 1½"

From the red stripe, cut:
- 11 strips, 1" x 42"
- 7 binding strips, 2" x 42"

From the large-scale floral print, cut:
- 4 strips, 5" x the lengthwise grain

SEW-AND-TRIM TECHNIQUES

Making Flying-Geese Units (page 12)
Half-Square-Triangle Units (page 10)
Trimming Units with Crossed Seams (page 13)
Making Units from Strip Sets (page 11)

MAKING THE BLOCKS

1. Sew two red 2½" squares and one ivory 2½" x 4½" rectangle together to make a flying-geese unit; press. Make 24 units.

Make 24.

2. Draw a diagonal line from corner to corner on the wrong side of each floral 4⅞" square. Place a marked floral square on a gold 4⅞" square, right sides together; stitch ¼" on each side of the drawn diagonal line. Cut and press. Make 12 half-square-triangle units, each 4½" x 4½".

Make 12.

3. Sew a gold 2½" square to one end of an ivory 2½" x 4½" rectangle to make a side unit. Press toward the gold square. Make 24 side units.

Make 24.

4. Sew one ivory 2½" square, one half-square-triangle unit from step 2, and two flying-geese units from step 1 together as shown; press. Make 12.

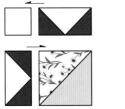

Make 12.

5. Sew two side units from step 3 to the unit from step 4 as shown; press. Trim the gold squares, leaving a ¼" seam allowance beyond the crossed seams.

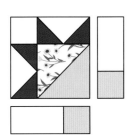 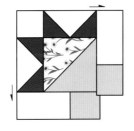

¼"

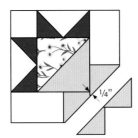

Make 12.

6. Fold an ivory triangle in half and lightly press to mark the center of the long side. Sew an ivory triangle to the unit from step 5, matching the center crease and the crossed seam. Press toward the ivory triangle. Make 12 basket units.

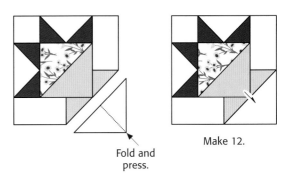

Fold and press.

Make 12.

7. Fold a basket unit in half vertically and horizontally and lightly crease to mark the center of each side. Fold four yellow-and-red print 6½" triangles in half and lightly crease to mark the center of the long side. Sew a triangle to opposite sides of basket unit, matching the center creases. Press the seams toward the triangles. Sew a triangle to the remaining sides to complete the block; press. Make 12 blocks.

Fold and press.

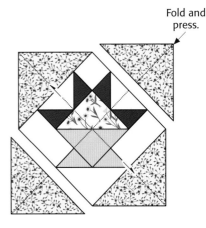

Make 12.

Piecing the Sashing

1. Sew two cream 1½" x 42" strips and one red stripe 1" x 42" strip together to a make a strip set. Press toward the cream strips. Make 11 strip sets. Cut 31 segments, each 11¾" wide.

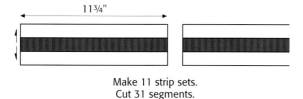

Make 11 strip sets.
Cut 31 segments.

2. Using a pencil and ruler, draw a diagonal line from corner to corner on the wrong side of each cream 1½" square. Place a marked cream square on opposite corners of a red 3" square with right sides together and raw edges aligned. Stitch directly on the drawn diagonal line. Trim away the excess fabric, leaving a ¼" seam allowance. Press the seams toward the cream triangle.

3. Place a marked cream square on each of the remaining corners of the red square, right sides together. Stitch directly on the drawn diagonal line. Trim away the excess fabric, leaving a ¼" seam allowance. Press the seams toward the cream triangle. Make 20 cornerstone units.

Make 20.

Quilt Top Assembly

1. Referring to "Assembling the Quilt Top" on pages 14–17, arrange the blocks and sashing units in rows. Sew four sashing units and three blocks together to make a block row. Press the seams toward the sashing units. Make four rows.

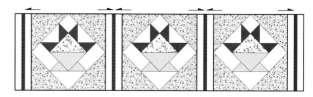

Make 4.

2. Sew four cornerstone units and three sashing units together to make a sashing row. Press the seams toward the sashing units. Make five rows.

Make 5.

3. Sew the block rows and sashing rows together. Press the seams toward the sashing rows.

ADDING THE BORDERS

For detailed instructions, refer to "Borders with Overlapped Corners" on pages 16–17.

1. Join the gold 1¼" inner-border strips end to end to make one continuous strip. Measure the quilt through the center from top to bottom and cut two border strips to fit that measurement.

2. Sew the trimmed gold strips to the side edges of the quilt top. Press toward the border strips.

3. Measure the quilt through the center from side to side, including the borders just added. Cut two gold border strips to fit that measurement.

4. Sew the trimmed gold strips to the top and bottom edges of the quilt top. Press toward the border strips.

5. Repeat steps 1–4 to measure, trim, and add the large-scale floral strips for the middle border. (You will not need to piece the strips.) Press toward the border strips.

6. Repeat steps 1–4 to measure, trim, and add the red 2" outer-border strips; press.

FINISHING THE QUILT

For detailed instructions on finishing techniques, refer to "Finishing" on pages 18–22.

1. Cut and piece the backing fabric so it is 4" to 6" larger than the quilt top. Layer the quilt top with batting and backing. Baste the layers together.

2. Hand or machine quilt as desired.

3. Square up the quilt sandwich.

4. Using the red 2" strips, prepare and sew the binding to the quilt. Add a hanging sleeve, if desired, and a label.

Quilting suggestions: Quilt a medallion in the center of each basket block and quilt a partial medallion in the large triangles. Quilt the sashing and borders in the ditch. Use a continuous design in the floral border.

Pieced and Quilted by Nancy Mahoney · Finished Quilt: 30¾" x 30¾" · Finished Block: 6"

Blue, yellow, and white form another timeless combination; these colors remind me of fresh blueberries and summer days. Can't you just picture this charming quilt on a special wall? This small quilt is so quick and easy, you can make one for yourself and one as a gift for a favorite friend.

MATERIALS

All yardages are based on 42"-wide fabric.

- ¾ yard of light print for block background and setting triangles
- ¾ yard of dark blue for blocks, sashing, border, and binding
- ⅝ yard of blue-and-yellow floral for border
- 1 fat quarter of medium blue for blocks
- 1 fat quarter of yellow for blocks
- 1 fat eighth of light blue for blocks
- 1¼ yards of fabric for backing
- 34" x 34" piece of batting

CUTTING

From the light blue, cut:
- 10 squares, 2" x 2"

From the dark blue, cut:
- 4 binding strips, 2" x 42"
- 4 strips, 1½" x 42"
- 3 strips, 1¼" x 42"; crosscut into 2 strips, 1¼" x 20", 4 rectangles, 1¼" x 8", and 6 rectangles, 1¼" x 6½"
- 10 squares, 2" x 2"

From the light print, cut:
- 2 strips, 2" x 42"; crosscut into 20 rectangles, 2" x 3½"
- 1 square, 12" x 12"; cut twice diagonally to yield 4 triangles
- 2 squares, 7" x 7"; cut once diagonally to yield 4 triangles
- 3 squares, 3⅞" x 3⅞"; cut once diagonally to yield 5 triangles (6 total; 1 is extra)
- 5 squares, 2" x 2"

From the yellow, cut:
- 10 squares, 2" x 2"
- 3 squares, 2⅜" x 2⅜"

From the medium blue, cut:
- 3 squares, 3⅞" x 3⅞"; cut once diagonally to yield 5 triangles (6 total; 1 is extra)
- 10 squares, 2" x 2"
- 3 squares, 2⅜" x 2⅜"

From the blue-and-yellow floral, cut:
- 4 strips, 4½" x 42"

SEW-AND-TRIM TECHNIQUES

Making Flying-Geese Units (page 12)
Half-Square-Triangle Units (page 10)
Trimming Units with Crossed Seams (page 13)

MAKING THE BLOCKS

1. Sew one light blue 2" square, one dark blue 2" square, and one light print 2" x 3½" rectangle together to make a flying-geese unit; press. Make five units and five reversed units.

Make 5.   Make 5.

2. Draw a diagonal line from corner to corner on the wrong side of each 2⅜" yellow square. Place a yellow square on a medium blue 2⅜" square, right sides together; stitch ¼" on each side of the drawn diagonal line. Cut and press. Make five half-square-triangle units, each 2" x 2". (You will have six total; one is extra.)

Make 5.

3. Sew two yellow 2" squares to one half-square-triangle unit from step 2. Press toward the yellow squares. Trim away the excess fabric, leaving a ¼" seam allowance beyond the crossed seams. Make five.

Make 5.

4. Sew one medium blue 3⅞" triangle and the unit from step 3 together to make a center unit. Press toward the blue triangle. Make five center units.

Make 5.

5. Sew a medium blue 2" square to one end of a light print 2" x 3½" rectangle to make a side unit. Press toward the blue square. Make 10 side units.

Make 10.

6. Sew one light print 2" square, one flying-geese unit from step 1, one reverse flying-geese unit from step 1, and one center unit from step 4 together as shown; press. Make five.

Make 5.

7. Sew two side units from step 5 to the unit from step 6 as shown; press. Trim the blue squares, leaving a ¼" seam allowance beyond the crossed seams. Make five.

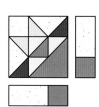 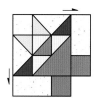

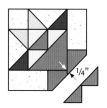

Make 5.

8. Fold a light print 3⅞" triangle in half and lightly press to mark the center of the long side. Sew the triangle to the unit from step 7, matching the center crease and the crossed seam to complete one block. Press toward the background triangle. Make five blocks.

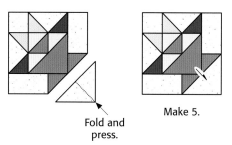

Fold and press.

Make 5.

QUILT TOP ASSEMBLY

1. Referring to "Assembling the Quilt Top" on pages 14–17, lay out the basket blocks and dark blue 1¼" sashing strips. Add the light print 12" side triangles.

2. Sew the blocks, sashing strips, and side triangles together in rows, pressing toward the sashing strips.

3. Sew the block rows and sashing strips together, pressing toward the sashing rows.

4. Add the light print 7" corner triangles; press toward the triangles.

5. Square up the quilt top, trimming the edges ¼"
   from the corners of the sashing as needed.

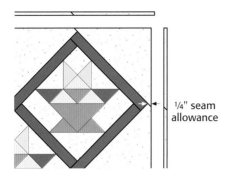

¼" seam
allowance

ADDING THE BORDERS

For detailed instructions, refer to "Borders with
Overlapped Corners" on pages 16–17.

1. Measure the quilt through the center from top to
   bottom and cut two dark blue 1½" inner-border
   strips to fit that measurement.

2. Sew the trimmed dark blue strips to the side
   edges of the quilt top. Press toward the border
   strips.

3. Measure the quilt through the center from side to
   side, including the borders just added. Cut two
   dark blue 1½" strips to fit that measurement.

4. Sew the trimmed dark blue strips to the top and
   bottom edges of the quilt top; press.

5. Repeat steps 1–4 to measure, trim, and add the
   floral 4½" outer-border strips; press.

FINISHING THE QUILT

For detailed instructions on finishing techniques, refer
to "Finishing" on pages 18–22.

1. Cut and piece the backing fabric so it is 4" to 6"
   larger than the quilt top. Layer the quilt top with
   batting and backing. Baste the layers together.

2. Hand or machine quilt as desired.

3. Square up the quilt sandwich.

4. Using the dark blue 2" strips, prepare and sew the
   binding to the quilt. Add a hanging sleeve, if
   desired, and a label.

Quilting suggestions: Quilt a partial medallion in the medium blue triangle of each basket
block and in the side and corner triangles.
Quilt the rest of the basket blocks, the sashing,
and the borders in the ditch. You can also quilt
a continuous design in the border.

Pieced and Quilted by Nancy Mahoney · Finished Quilt: 56½" x 56½" · Finished Block: 10"

In this quilt, the simplicity of the colors makes the design particularly striking; the yellow creates a golden glow and provides a nice foil for the purple and green. The basket blocks almost disappear in the side-by-side setting, producing a wonderful secondary design, which is further enhanced by the simple pieced border.

MATERIALS

All yardages are based on 42"-wide fabric.

- 2⅜ yards of purple print for blocks, border, and binding
- 1⅞ yards of yellow print for blocks and border
- ¾ yard of green print for blocks
- ½ yard of pear print for blocks
- 3¾ yards of fabric for backing
- 60" x 60" piece of batting

CUTTING

From the purple print, cut:

- 1 strip, 8" x 42"; crosscut into 4 squares, 8" x 8"
- 6 binding strips, 2" x 42"

From the remaining purple print, cut:

- 4 strips, 3½" x the lengthwise grain
- 16 squares, 5⅞" x 5⅞"
- 64 squares, 2½" x 2½"
- 4 squares, 5½" x 5½"

From the yellow print, cut:

- 1 strip, 8" x 42"; crosscut into 4 squares, 8" x 8"
- 3 strips, 5⅞" x 42"; crosscut into 16 squares, 5⅞" x 5⅞"
- 1 strip, 4⅞" x 42"; crosscut into 8 squares, 4⅞" x 4⅞"; cut each square once diagonally to yield 16 triangles
- 6 strips, 2½" x 42"; crosscut into 32 rectangles, 2½" x 6½"
- 4 strips, 2½" x 42"; crosscut into 32 rectangles, 2½" x 4½"
- 1 strip, 2½" x 42"; crosscut into 16 squares, 2½" x 2½"

From the pear print, cut:

- 2 strips, 6⅞" x 42"; crosscut into 8 squares, 6⅞" x 6⅞"

From the green print, cut:

- 2 strips, 6⅞" x 42"; crosscut into 8 squares, 6⅞" x 6⅞"
- 2 strips, 2½" x 42"; crosscut into 32 squares, 2½" x 2½"

SEW-AND-TRIM TECHNIQUES

Multiple Half-Square-Triangle Units (page 9)
Making Flying-Geese Units (page 12)
Half-Square-Triangle Units (page 10)
Trimming Units with Crossed Seams (page 13)

MAKING THE BLOCKS

1. Pair each purple 8" square with each yellow 8" square, right sides facing up. Cut and piece 2½"-wide bias strips. Make eight strip sets. Cut 32 half-square-triangle units, each 2½" x 2½".

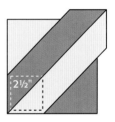

Make 8 strip sets.
Cut 32 units.

2. Sew two purple 2½" squares and one yellow 2½" x 4½" rectangle together to make a flying-geese unit; press. Make 32 units.

Make 32.

3. Draw a diagonal line from corner to corner on the wrong side of each pear print 6⅞" square. Place a pear print square on a green 6⅞" square, right sides together; stitch ¼" on each side of the drawn diagonal line. Cut and press toward the green triangle. Make 16 half-square-triangle units, each 6½" x 6½".

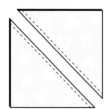

Make 16.

4. Sew a green 2½" square to one end of a yellow 2½" x 6½" rectangle to make a side unit. Press toward the green square. Make 32 side units.

Make 32.

5. Sew one yellow 2½" square, two half-square-triangle units from step 1, one half-square-triangle unit from step 3, and two flying-geese units from step 2 together as shown. Press. Make 16.

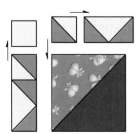

Make 16.

6. Sew two side units from step 4 to the unit from step 5 as shown; press. Trim the green squares, leaving a ¼" seam allowance beyond the crossed seams. Make 16.

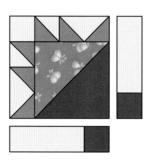

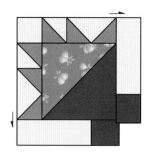

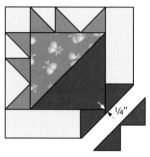

Make 16.

7. Fold a yellow 4⅞" triangle in half and lightly press to mark the center of the long side. Sew a yellow triangle to the unit from step 6, matching the center crease and the crossed seam to complete one block. Press toward the yellow triangle. Make 16 blocks.

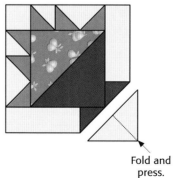

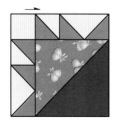

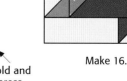

Fold and press.

Make 16.

QUILT TOP ASSEMBLY

1. Referring to "Assembling the Quilt Top" on pages 14–17, arrange and sew the blocks in four rows of four blocks each, rotating the blocks as shown in the quilt diagram; press.

2. Sew the rows together; press. The quilt top should measure 40½" x 40½", including seam allowances, for the outer pieced border to fit correctly.

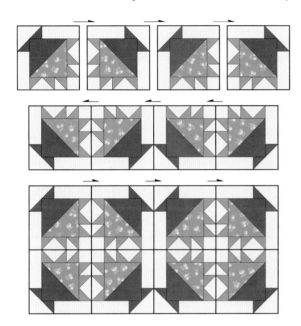

ADDING THE BORDERS

1. Draw a diagonal line from corner to corner on the wrong side of each yellow 5⅞" square. Place a yellow square on a purple 5⅞" square, right sides together; stitch ¼" on each side of the drawn diagonal line. Cut and press toward the purple triangle. Make 32 half-square-triangle units, each 5½" x 5½".

Make 32.

2. Arrange and sew eight half-square-triangle units together as shown to make a side border row; press. Make two.

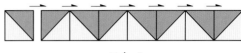

Make 2.

3. Arrange and sew eight half-square-triangle units and two purple 5½" squares together as shown to make a top border row; press. Repeat to make a bottom border row.

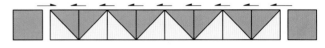

Make 2.

4. Sew the border rows from step 2 to the side edges of the quilt top. Press toward the border rows.

5. Sew the border rows from step 3 to the top and bottom edges of the quilt top. Press toward the border rows.

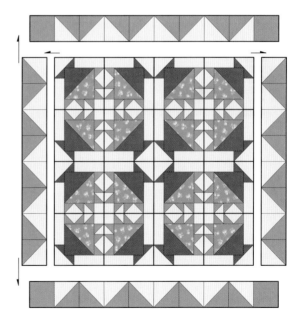

6. Measure the quilt through the center from top to bottom and cut two purple 3½" outer-border strips to fit that measurement. For detailed instructions, refer to "Borders with Overlapped Corners" on pages 16–17.

7. Sew the trimmed border strips to the side edges of the quilt top. Press toward the border strips.

8. Measure the quilt through the center from side to side, including the borders just added. Cut two purple 3½" border strips to that measurement.

9. Sew the trimmed purple border strips to the top and bottom edges of the quilt top; press.

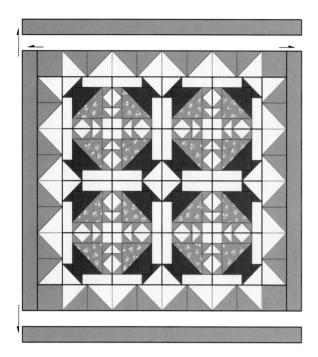

FINISHING THE QUILT

For detailed instructions on finishing techniques, refer to "Finishing" on pages 18–22.

1. Cut and piece the backing fabric so it is 4" to 6" larger than the quilt top. Layer the quilt top with batting and backing. Baste the layers together.

2. Hand or machine quilt as desired.

3. Square up the quilt sandwich.

4. Using the purple 2" strips, prepare and sew the binding to the quilt. Add a hanging sleeve, if desired, and a label.

Quilting suggestions: Quilt a partial medallion in the pear triangle of the basket blocks; stitch radiating lines in the green triangle. Quilt medallion designs and straight lines that echo the zigzag piecing in the borders. Add a straight line of stitching in the purple border about 1" from the outside edge.

DESIGN OPTION

The quilt shown below illustrates another design option. Thirteen blocks are set in a diagonal setting with a floral print in the setting triangles. The pink inner border frames the center design and a large-scale floral outer border completes the look of this romantic quilt.

MONTICELLO BASKETS
Pieced and Quilted by Nancy Mahoney

Pieced and Quilted by Nancy Mahoney · Finished Quilt: 32" x 32" · Finished Block: 8⅛"

The bright, clear colors in the fanciful floral print used in the borders of this quilt remind me of a sunny spring day. Not only does this traditional quilt have an updated look, but the basket block is also made using new, easy-to-construct techniques. Celebrate spring all year long with this delightful quilt. See the antique quilt that inspired "Spring Baskets" on page 4.

MATERIALS

All yardages are based on 42"-wide fabric.

- 1 yard of blue floral print for setting triangles and borders
- 1 yard of blue tone-on-tone print for blocks and binding
- ¾ yard of light print for block background
- ¼ yard of yellow print for inner border
- 1¼ yards of fabric for backing
- 36" x 36" piece of batting
- Fusible web

CUTTING

From the light print, cut:
- 3 squares, 9" x 9"; cut once diagonally to yield 5 triangles (6 total; 1 is extra)
- 1 square, 9" x 9"
- 3 squares, 4⅛" x 4⅛"
- 10 rectangles, 2⅛" x 5¾"
- 5 squares, 2⅛" x 2⅛"

From the blue tone-on-tone print, cut:
- 1 square, 9" x 9"
- 3 squares, 4⅛" x 4⅛"
- 15 squares, 2⅛" x 2⅛"
- 4 binding strips, 2" x 42"

From the blue floral print, cut:
- 4 strips, 4" x 42"
- 1 square, 13¼" x 13¼"; cut twice diagonally to yield 4 triangles
- 2 squares, 7" x 7"; cut once diagonally to yield 4 triangles

From the yellow print, cut:
- 4 strips, 1¼" x 42"

SEW-AND-TRIM TECHNIQUES

Multiple Half-Square-Triangle Units (page 9)
Half-Square-Triangle Units (page 10)
Trimming Units with Crossed Seams (page 13)

MAKING THE BLOCKS

1. Pair the light print 9" square with the blue tone-on-tone 9" square, right sides facing up. Cut and piece 2¼"-wide bias strips. Make two strip sets. Cut 10 half-square-triangle units, each 2⅛" x 2⅛".

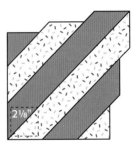

Make 2 strip sets.
Cut 10 units.

2. Draw a diagonal line from corner to corner on the wrong side of each light print 4⅛" square. Place a light print square on a blue tone-on-tone 4⅛" square, right sides together; stitch ¼" on each side of the drawn line. Cut and press toward the blue triangle. Make five half-square-triangle units, each 3¾" x 3¾". (You will have six total; one is extra.)

Make 5.

3. Draw a diagonal line from corner to corner on the wrong side of each light print 2⅛" square. Place a light print square on the blue corner of a half-square-triangle unit from step 2, with right sides together and raw edges aligned. Stitch directly on the drawn line. Trim away the excess fabric, leaving a ¼" seam allowance. Press toward the light print. Make five.

Make 5.

4. Sew a blue tone-on-tone 2⅛" square to each of the half-square-triangle units from step 1. Make 10 of these units.

Make 10.

5. Arrange and sew two units from step 4, one unit from step 3, one blue tone-on-tone 2⅛" square, and two light print 2⅛" x 5¾" rectangles together as shown; press. Trim away the excess fabric, leaving a ¼" seam allowance beyond the crossed seams. Make five.

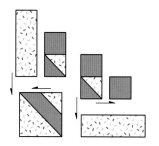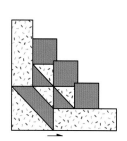

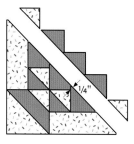

Make 5.

6. Use the pattern on page 58 to make a template for the basket handle appliqué. Follow the manufacturer's instructions to trace five basket handles onto the fusible web and then fuse the web to the wrong side of the remaining blue tone-on-tone fabric. Cut out the basket handles right on the line. Fold each light print 9" triangle in half and lightly crease to mark the center of the long side. Fold each basket handle in half and lightly crease to mark the center. Position the basket handle on each triangle, matching the center creases. Fuse the basket handles to the triangles.

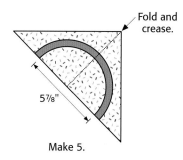

Fold and crease.

5⅞"

Make 5.

7. Stitch around the edges of each basket handle using matching thread and a machine straight, zigzag, or blanket stitch.

8. Sew the basket unit from step 5 to the handle from step 7 to complete the block; press. Trim the block as needed to measure 8⅝" x 8⅝". Make five blocks.

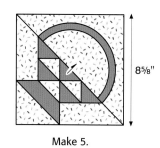

8⅝"

Make 5.

QUILT TOP ASSEMBLY

1. Referring to "Assembling the Quilt Top" on pages 14–17, lay out the basket blocks. Add the blue floral 13¼" side triangles.

2. Sew the blocks and side triangles together in rows, following the direction of the arrows in the diagram for pressing.

3. Sew the rows together, adding the blue floral 7" corner triangles last. Press the seams toward the blue floral.

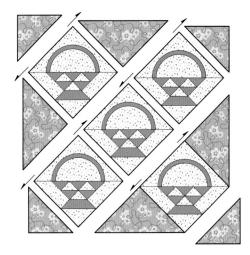

4. Square up the quilt top, trimming the edges ¼" from the corners of the blocks.

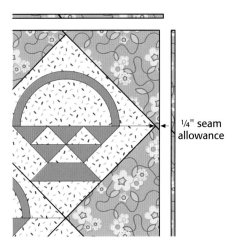

¼" seam allowance

ADDING THE BORDERS

For detailed instructions, refer to "Borders with Overlapped Corners" on pages 16–17.

1. Measure the quilt through the center from top to bottom and cut two yellow 1¼" inner-border strips to fit that measurement.

2. Sew the trimmed inner-border strips to the side edges of the quilt top. Press toward the border strips.

3. Measure the quilt through the center from side to side, including the borders just added. Cut two yellow 1¼" inner-border strips to fit that measurement.

4. Sew the trimmed inner-border strips to the top and bottom edges of the quilt top; press toward the border.

5. Repeat steps 1–4 to measure, trim, and add the floral print 4" outer-border strips. Press toward the border strips.

FINISHING THE QUILT

For detailed instructions on finishing techniques, refer to "Finishing" on pages 18–22.

1. Cut the backing fabric so it is 4" to 6" larger than the quilt top. Layer the quilt top with batting and backing. Baste the layers together.

2. Hand or machine quilt as desired.

3. Square up the quilt sandwich.

4. Using the blue tone-on-tone 2" strips, prepare and sew the binding to the quilt. Add a hanging sleeve, if desired, and a label.

Quilting suggestions: Quilt each basket in the ditch and stitch a floral medallion in the background between the basket and handle. Quilt a partial medallion in the side and corner triangles. Quilt a continuous design in the border and quilt the narrow borders in the ditch.

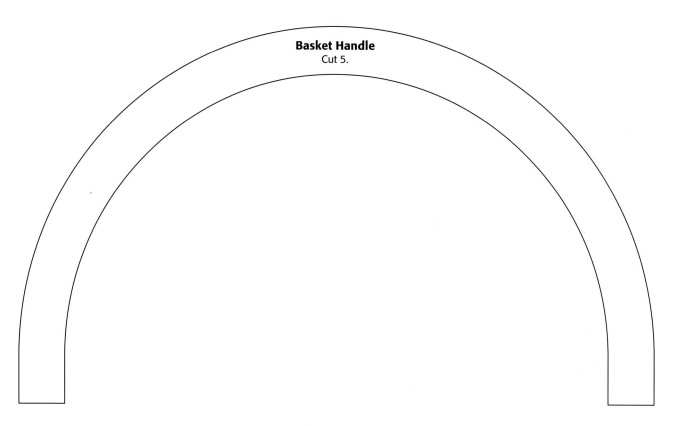

Basket Handle
Cut 5.

Pieced and Quilted by Nancy Mahoney · Finished Quilt: 58¼" x 58¼" · Finished Block: 10"

Red-and-white quilts share the same legacy as basket quilts—both have been a favorite of quilters for over a hundred and fifty years. In this updated version, the pieced border softens the edges while the light background print adds a romantic touch. The results give this quilt the charm of yesteryear with a contemporary twist.

MATERIALS

All yardages are based on 42"-wide fabric.

- 2⅜ yards of red swirl print for blocks, border, and binding
- 2⅛ yards of red-and-white large-scale floral background print for block background, setting squares, setting triangles, and border
- 1 fat quarter *each* of 6 red prints for blocks
- 1 fat quarter *each* of 6 red-and-white small-scale background prints for blocks
- 3⅞ yards of fabric for backing
- 63" x 63" piece of batting

CUTTING

From *each* of the 6 red-and-white small-scale background prints, cut:
- 2 squares, 8" x 8" (12 total)
- 4 squares, 2½" x 2½" (24 total)

From *each* of the 6 red prints, cut:
- 2 squares, 8" x 8" (12 total)

From the red-and-white large-scale floral background print, cut:
- 3 strips, 4⅝" x 42"; crosscut into 12 rectangles, 4⅝" x 8⅜"
- 3 strips, 2½" x 42"; crosscut into 18 rectangles, 2½" x 6½"
- 2 squares, 16" x 16"; cut twice diagonally to yield 8 triangles
- 4 squares, 10½" x 10½"
- 2 squares, 8⅜" x 8⅜"; cut once diagonally to yield 4 triangles
- 5 squares, 4⅞" x 4⅞"; cut once diagonally to yield 9 triangles (10 total; 1 is extra)
- 3 squares, 2½" x 2½"

From the red swirl print, cut:
- 7 binding strips, 2" x 42"
- 2 strips, 2½" x 42"; crosscut into 18 squares, 2½" x 2½"

From the remaining red swirl print, cut:
- 4 strips, 4" x the lengthwise grain
- 5 squares, 6⅞" x 6⅞"; cut once diagonally to yield 9 triangles (10 total; 1 is extra)
- 12 rectangles, 4⅝" x 8⅜"
- 4 squares, 4½" x 4½"

SEW-AND-TRIM TECHNIQUES

Multiple Half-Square-Triangle Units (page 9)
Trimming Units with Crossed Seams (page 13)

MAKING THE BLOCKS

1. Pair each small-scale background 8" square with a red print 8" square, right sides facing up. Cut and piece 2½"-wide bias strips. Make 24 strip sets. Cut 90 half-square-triangle units, each 2½" x 2½".

**Make 24 strip sets.
Cut 90 units.**

2. Sew three units from step 1 and three large-scale or small-scale background 2½" squares together in rows as shown; press. Sew the rows together and press. Trim away the excess fabric, leaving a ¼" seam allowance beyond the crossed seams. Make nine.

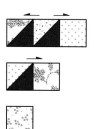
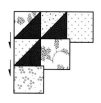

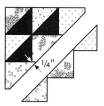

Make 9.

3. Sew a red swirl 6⅞" triangle to the unit from step 2; press. Make nine.

Make 9.

4. Sew seven half-square-triangle units from step 1 and the unit from step 3 together as shown; press. Make nine.

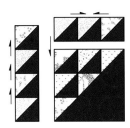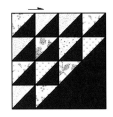

Make 9.

5. Sew a red swirl 2½" square to one end of a large-scale floral background 2½" x 6½" rectangle to make a side unit. Press toward the red square. Make 18 side units.

Make 18.

6. Sew two side units from step 5 to the unit from step 4 as shown; press. Trim the red squares, leaving a ¼" seam allowance beyond the crossed seams. Make nine.

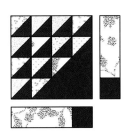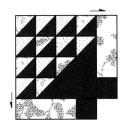

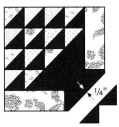

Make 9.

7. Fold a large-scale floral background 4⅞" triangle in half and lightly press to mark the center of the long side. Sew the triangle to the unit from step 6, matching the center crease and the crossed seam to complete one block. Press toward the background triangle. Make nine blocks.

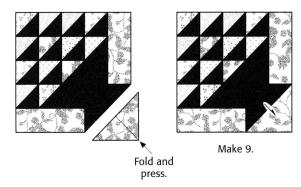

Fold and press.

Make 9.

QUILT TOP ASSEMBLY

1. Referring to "Assembling the Quilt Top" on pages 14–17, lay out the Basket blocks and large-scale floral 10½" setting squares. Add the large-scale floral 16" side triangles.

2. Sew the blocks, setting squares, and side triangles together in rows. Press toward the floral setting squares and triangles.

3. Sew the rows together, adding the large-scale floral 8⅜" corner triangles last. Press toward the corner setting triangles.

4. Square up the quilt top, trimming the edges ⅜" from the corners of the blocks as needed. The quilt top should measure 43¼" x 43¼", including seam allowances, for the pieced borders to fit correctly.

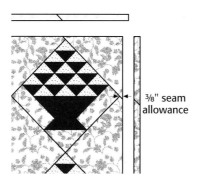

⅜" seam allowance

ADDING THE BORDERS

1. Using a rotary cutter and ruler, cut the red swirl and large-scale floral background 4⅝" x 8⅜" rectangles as shown to yield 12 floral background triangles, 12 reversed floral background triangles, 12 red swirl triangles, and 12 reversed red swirl triangles.

Cut 6 to make 12 triangles.　　Cut 6 to make 12 triangles.

Cut 6 to make 12 triangles.　　Cut 6 to make 12 triangles.

2. Arrange the red swirl and floral background triangles from step 1 in pairs, offsetting the points as shown, and sew; press. Make 12 rectangle units and 12 reversed rectangle units, each 4½" x 7⅝".

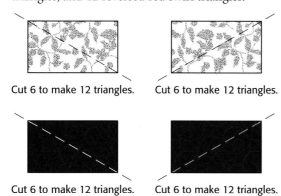

½"

½"

Make 12.　　　　　Make 12.

3. Sew three units and three reversed units from step 2 together to make a border row as shown; press. Make four border rows.

Make 4.

4. Sew a border row to the side edges of the quilt top. Press toward the center.

5. Sew a red swirl 4½" square to each end of the two remaining border rows. Sew the border rows to the top and bottom edges of the quilt top. Press toward the center.

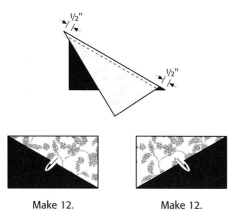

6. Measure the quilt through the center from top to bottom and cut two red swirl 4" outer-border strips to fit that measurement. Refer to "Borders with Overlapped Corners" on pages 16–17 for detailed instructions.

7. Sew the trimmed border strips to the side edges of the quilt top. Press toward the border strips.

8. Measure the quilt through the center from side to side, including the borders just added. Cut two red swirl 4" outer-border strips to fit that measurement.

9. Sew the trimmed outer-border strips to the top and bottom edges of the quilt top; press.

FINISHING THE QUILT

For detailed instructions on finishing techniques, refer to "Finishing" on pages 18–22.

1. Cut and piece the backing fabric so it is 4" to 6" larger than the quilt top. Layer the quilt top with batting and backing. Baste the layers together.

2. Hand or machine quilt as desired.

3. Square up the quilt.

4. Using the red swirl 2" strips, prepare and sew the binding to the quilt. Add a hanging sleeve, if desired, and a label.

Quilting suggestions: Quilt each basket in the ditch. Quilt a medallion pattern in the large setting squares. Quilt a partial medallion in the side triangles and the background of the pieced border to make a continuous design. Repeat the partial medallion in the red part of the pieced border. Quilt a continuous design in the border.

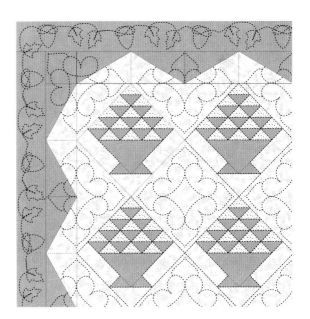

Pieced and Quilted by Nancy Mahoney · Finished Quilt: 64½" x 64½" · Finished Block: 10"

A magnificent secondary design of blue stars within red stars is created when these intriguing basket blocks are set in straight rows. The intricate-looking checkerboard border (which isn't at all difficult) completes the design. This spectacular quilt would be a marvelous accent anywhere in your home.

MATERIALS

All yardages are based on 42"-wide fabric.

- 3¼ yards of beige print for blocks and borders
- 2⅜ yards of blue floral print for borders
- ⅞ yard of red print for blocks and borders
- ⅞ yard of small-scale blue print for blocks
- ¾ yard of blue-and-green print for blocks
- ½ yard of gold stripe for binding
- 4¼ yards of fabric for backing
- 68" x 68" piece of batting

CUTTING

From the beige print, cut:

- 2 strips, 11" x 42"; crosscut into 4 squares, 11" x 11", and 2 squares, 8" x 8"
- 1 strip, 4⅞" x 42"; crosscut into 8 squares, 4⅞" x 4⅞"; cut each square once diagonally to yield 16 triangles
- 6 strips, 2½" x 42"; crosscut into 32 rectangles, 2½" x 6½"
- 4 strips, 2½" x 42"; crosscut into 32 rectangles, 2½" x 4½"
- 4 strips, 2½" x 42"; crosscut into 64 squares, 2½" x 2½"
- 12 strips, 2" x 42"
- 1 strip, 2" x 42"; crosscut into 4 rectangles, 2" x 10"
- 11 strips, 1½" x 42"

From the red print, cut:

- 2 strips, 2½" x 42"; crosscut into 32 squares, 2½" x 2½"
- 6 strips, 2" x 42"
- 2 rectangles, 2" x 10"
- 2 squares, 8" x 8"

From the small-scale blue print, cut:

- 2 strips, 2½" x 42"; crosscut into 32 squares, 2½" x 2½"
- 4 squares, 11" x 11"

From the blue-and-green print, cut:

- 2 strips, 2½" x 42"; crosscut into 32 squares, 2½" x 2½"
- 8 squares, 6⅞" x 6⅞"; cut once diagonally to yield 16 triangles

From the blue floral print, cut:

- 6 strips, 2" x 42"

From the remaining blue floral print, cut:

- 4 strips, 4½" x the lengthwise grain
- 2 rectangles, 2" x 10"

From the gold stripe, cut:

- 7 binding strips, 2" x 42"

SEW-AND-TRIM TECHNIQUES

Multiple Half-Square-Triangle Units (page 9)
Making Flying-Geese Units (page 12)
Trimming Units with Crossed Seams (page 13)
Making Units from Strip Sets (page 11)

MAKING THE BLOCKS

1. Pair each beige 8" square with each red 8" square, right sides facing up. Cut and piece 2½"-wide bias strips. Make four strip sets. Cut 16 half-square-triangle units, each 2½" x 2½".

Make 4 strip sets.
Cut 16 units.

2. Pair each beige 11" square with each small-scale blue 11" square, right sides facing up. Cut and piece 2½"-wide bias strips. Make eight strip sets. Cut 64 half-square-triangle units, each 2½" x 2½".

Make 8 strip sets.
Cut 64 units.

3. Sew a red 2½" square, a small-scale blue 2½" square, and a beige 2½" x 4½" rectangle together to make one flying-geese unit; press. Make 16 flying-geese units and 16 reversed flying-geese units.

Make 16.   Make 16.

4. Sew one half-square-triangle unit from step 1, two half-square-triangle units from step 2, and three beige 2½" squares together in rows as shown; press. Sew the rows together and press. Trim away the excess fabric, leaving a ¼" seam allowance beyond the crossed seams. Make 16.

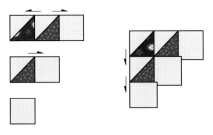

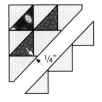

Make 16.

5. Sew a blue-and-green 6⅞" triangle to the unit from step 4; press. Make 16.

Make 16.

6. Sew two half-square-triangle units from step 2, one unit from step 3, one reversed unit from step 3, the unit from step 5, and one beige 2½" square together as shown; press. Make 16.

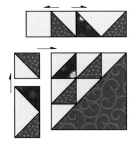 

Make 16.

7. Sew a blue-and-green 2½" square to one end of a beige 2½" x 6½" rectangle to make a side unit. Press toward the blue-and-green square. Make 32 side units.

Make 32.

8. Sew two side units from step 7 to the unit from step 6 as shown; press. Trim the blue-and-green squares, leaving a ¼" seam allowance beyond the crossed seams. Make 16.

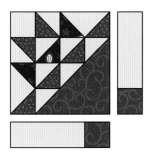

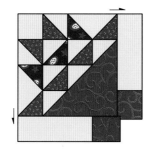

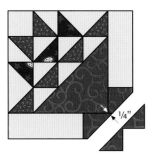

Make 16.

9. Fold a beige 4⅞" triangle in half and lightly press to mark the center of the long side. Sew the triangle to the unit from step 8, matching the center crease and the crossed seam to complete one block. Press toward the beige triangle. Make 16 blocks.

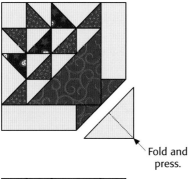

Fold and press.

Make 16.

QUILT TOP ASSEMBLY

1. Referring to "Assembling the Quilt Top" on pages 14–17, arrange and sew the blocks in four rows of four blocks each, rotating the blocks as shown; press.

2. Sew the rows together; press. The quilt top should measure 40½" x 40½", including seam allowances.

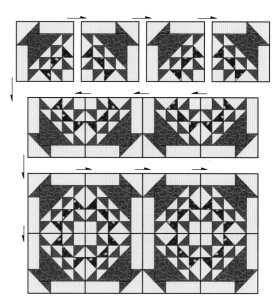

ADDING THE BORDERS

1. Sew five beige 1½" x 42" border strips together end to end to make one continuous strip. Measure the quilt through the center from top to bottom and cut two inner-border strips to fit that measurement. Refer to "Borders with Overlapped Corners" on pages 16–17 for further details.

2. Sew the trimmed beige inner-border strips to the side edges of the quilt top. Press toward the border strips.

3. Measure the quilt through the center from side to side, including the borders just added. Cut two beige inner-border strips to fit that measurement.

4. Sew the trimmed inner-border strips to the top and bottom edges of the quilt top; press. The quilt top should measure 42½" x 42½", including seam allowances.

5. Sew two beige 2" x 42" strips, one blue floral 2" x 42" strip, and one red 2" x 42" strip together to make strip set A. Press as shown. Make six strip sets. Cut the strips into 120 segments, each 2" wide.

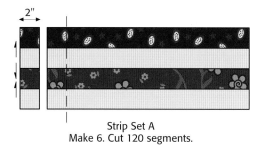

Strip Set A
Make 6. Cut 120 segments.

6. Sew the beige, blue floral, and red 2" x 10" rectangles together in the combinations shown to make strip sets B and C. Press as shown. Cut each strip set into four segments, each 2" wide.

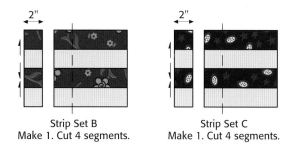

Strip Set B
Make 1. Cut 4 segments.

Strip Set C
Make 1. Cut 4 segments.

7. Sew 28 segments from strip set A together, rotating the segments as shown, to make a border row. Press all of the seams in one direction. Make two border rows; label these border row A for the top and bottom borders. Make two reversed border rows; label these border row B for the side borders.

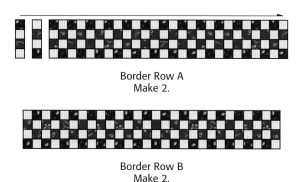

Border Row A
Make 2.

Border Row B
Make 2.

8. Sew two segments from strip set A, one segment from strip B, and one segment from strip set C together in the combinations shown. Press as shown. Make two blocks of each and label them corner block C and corner block D.

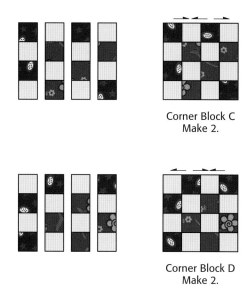

Corner Block C
Make 2.

Corner Block D
Make 2.

9. Sew the B border rows to the side edges of the quilt top. Press toward the beige inner border.

10. Sew a corner block to each end of the A border rows as shown. Press the seam allowance toward the corner blocks. Sew the border rows to the top and bottom edges of the quilt top. Press toward the beige border.

11. Sew six beige 1½" x 42" strips together to make one continuous strip. Repeat steps 1–4 (on page 67) to measure, trim, and add the inner-border strips. Press toward the border strips.

12. Repeat steps 1–4 to measure, trim, and add the blue floral 4½" outer-border strips. (You will not need to piece these strips.) Press toward the border strips.

FINISHING THE QUILT

For detailed instructions on finishing techniques, refer to "Finishing" on pages 18–22.

1. Cut and piece the backing fabric so it is 4" to 6" larger than the quilt top. Layer the quilt top with batting and backing. Baste the layers together.

2. Hand or machine quilt as desired.

3. Square up the quilt sandwich.

4. Using the gold stripe 2" strips, prepare and sew the binding to the quilt. Add a hanging sleeve, if desired, and a label.

Quilting suggestions: Quilt a rectangular medallion design in the rectangles between the blocks and a square medallion in the center of the stars and in the center background square. Quilt a partial medallion in the large blue triangle in the basket block and in the background triangle on the sides where the blocks meet. Quilt the pieced border in the ditch and use a continuous design in the outer border.

Pieced and Quilted by Nancy Mahoney · Finished Quilt: 55½" x 55¾" · Finished Block: 8"

The green floral print and pink baskets bring back memories of my grandmother's flower garden and green her lawn chairs. The basket blocks are simple to piece, and the strippy-style setting is perfect for showcasing a favorite large-scale print. Add a little nostalgia to any decor with this charming quilt.

MATERIALS

All yardages are based on 42"-wide fabric.

- 1¾ yards of large-scale green floral for borders
- 1⅜ yards of pink print for blocks, sashing, and binding
- 1⅛ yards of small-scale floral for setting triangles
- ⅞ yard of cream print for block backgrounds
- ⅜ yard of yellow plaid for blocks
- 3⅝ yards of fabric for backing
- 60" x 60" piece of batting

CUTTING

From the pink print, cut:
- 10 strips, 1½" x 42"
- 6 binding strips, 2" x 42"
- 5 strips, 2½" x 42"; crosscut into 72 squares, 2½" x 2½"

From the cream print, cut:
- 1 strip, 4⅞" x 42"; crosscut into 6 squares, 4⅞" x 4⅞"; cut each square once diagonally to yield 12 triangles
- 6 strips, 2½" x 42"; crosscut into 48 rectangles, 2½" x 4½"
- 2 strips, 2½" x 42"; crosscut into 24 squares, 2½" x 2½"

From the yellow plaid, cut:
- 1 strip, 4⅞" x 42"; crosscut into 6 squares, 4⅞" x 4⅞"; cut each square once diagonally to yield 12 triangles
- 2 strips, 2½" x 42"; crosscut into 24 squares, 2½" x 2½"

From the small-scale floral, cut:
- 2 strips, 13" x 42"; crosscut into 5 squares, 13" x 13"; cut each square twice diagonally to yield 18 triangles (20 total; 2 are extra)
- 1 strip, 7" x 42"; crosscut into 6 squares, 7" x 7"; cut each square once diagonally to yield 12 triangles

From the large-scale green floral, cut:
- 2 strips, 4" x the lengthwise grain
- 4 strips, 4½" x the lengthwise grain

SEW-AND-TRIM TECHNIQUES

Making Flying-Geese Units (page 12)
Trimming Units with Crossed Seams (page 13)
Making Units from Strip Sets (page 11)

MAKING THE BLOCKS

1. Sew two pink 2½" squares and a cream 2½" x 4½" rectangle together to make a flying-geese unit; press. Make 24 units.

Make 24.

2. Sew two pink 2½" squares and one cream 2½" square together as shown. Press toward the pink squares. Trim away the excess fabric, leaving a ¼" seam allowance beyond the crossed seams. Make 12.

Make 12.

3. Sew one yellow plaid 4⅞" triangle and the unit from step 2 together to make a center unit. Press toward the yellow triangle. Make 12 center units.

Make 12.

4. Sew a yellow plaid 2½" square to one end of a cream 2½" x 4½" rectangle to make a side unit. Press toward the yellow square. Make 24 side units.

Make 24.

5. Sew one cream 2½" square, two flying-geese units from step 1, and one center unit from step 3 together as shown. Press as shown. Make 12.

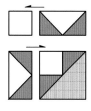

Make 12.

6. Sew two side units from step 4 to the unit from step 5 as shown; press. Trim the yellow squares, leaving a ¼" seam allowance beyond the crossed seams. Make 12.

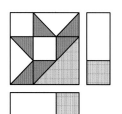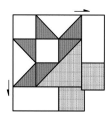

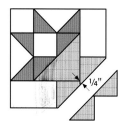

¼"

Make 12.

7. Fold a cream 4⅞" triangle in half and lightly press to mark the center of the long side. Sew the triangle to the unit from step 6, matching the center crease and the crossed seam to complete one block. Press toward the cream triangle. Make 12 blocks.

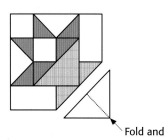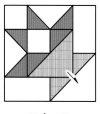

Fold and press.

Make 12.

QUILT TOP ASSEMBLY

1. Assemble and sew four basket blocks and six small-scale floral 13" side triangles into a vertical row as shown; press.

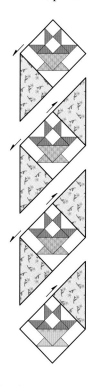

2. Sew the four small-scale floral 7" corner triangles on last; press. Repeat to make three vertical rows.

Make 3.

3. Square up each row by trimming the excess tri-angle fabric, leaving a ¼" seam allowance all the way around the pieced strip.

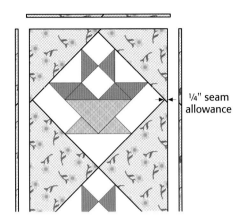

¼" seam allowance

4. Measure the length of all three vertical rows. If they differ, estimate the average and consider this the length. Sew seven of the pink 1½" x 42" strips together end to end to make a continuous strip. From this long strip, cut six sashing strips the length of your measurement.

5. Make a strip set from the trimmed pink sashing and the large-scale floral 4" strips. Trim the two large-scale floral strips to the same length as the vertical basket rows. Sew a pink sashing strip to each long side of the floral strip. Press toward the pink strips. Make two.

Make 2.

6. Sew the basket rows, the two strip sets from step 5, and the two remaining pink strips from step 4 together as shown. Press toward the pink strips.

ADDING THE BORDERS

For detailed instructions, refer to "Borders with Overlapped Corners" on pages 16–17.

1. Sew the remaining three 1½" x 42" pink border strips together end to end to make one continu-ous strip. Measure the quilt through the center from side to side and cut two border strips to fit that measurement.

2. Sew the trimmed pink border strips to the top and bottom edges of the quilt top; press toward the border strips.

3. Measure the quilt through the center from top to bottom and cut two large-scale floral 4½" outer border strips to fit that measurement.

4. Sew the trimmed outer-border strips to the side edges of the quilt top. Press toward the border strips.

5. Measure the quilt through the center from side to side, including the borders just added. Cut two large-scale floral 4½" outer-border strips to fit that measurement.

6. Sew the trimmed outer-border strips to the top and bottom edges of the quilt top; press.

FINISHING THE QUILT

For detailed instructions on finishing techniques, refer to "Finishing" on pages 18–22.

1. Cut and piece the backing fabric so it is 4" to 6" larger than the quilt top. Layer the quilt top with batting and backing. Baste the layers together.

2. Hand or machine quilt as desired.

3. Square up the quilt sandwich.

4. Using the pink 2"-wide strips, prepare and sew the binding to the quilt. Add a hanging sleeve, if desired, and a label.

Quilting suggestions: Quilt each basket block in the ditch and quilt a cross-hatch design in the yellow basket triangle. Quilt a partial medallion in the side and corner triangles. Quilt the narrow pink strips in the ditch and quilt a continuous design in the vertical floral strips and border.

Pieced and Quilted by Nancy Mahoney · Finished Quilt: 58" x 71½" · Finished Block: 12"

While the design in this stunning quilt looks intricate, the blocks are easy to piece. A light background floral print and complementary fabrics create layers of texture and visual impact. Whether you hang it on a special wall or cuddle up with it in a favorite chair, enjoy this lasting garden of roses all year long.

MATERIALS

All yardages are based on 42"-wide fabric.

- 2 yards of green print for blocks, borders, and binding
- 1⅝ yards of large-scale floral print for blocks, sashing, and borders
- 1⅜ yards of purple print for blocks and border
- ⅞ yard of cream print for block backgrounds
- ⅜ yard of pink print for blocks
- ⅜ yard of yellow print for blocks and sashing squares
- 1 fat quarter of a coordinating floral print for blocks
- 3⅞ yards of fabric for backing
- 62" x 76" piece of batting

CUTTING

From the pink print, cut:
- 4 strips, 2⅝" x 42"; crosscut into 48 squares, 2⅝" x 2⅝"

From the cream print, cut:
- 1 strip, 5⅛" x 42"; crosscut into 6 squares, 5⅛" x 5⅛"; cut each square once diagonally to yield 12 triangles
- 6 strips, 2⅝" x 42"; crosscut into 48 rectangles, 2⅝" x 4¾"
- 1 strip, 2⅝" x 42"; crosscut into 12 squares, 2⅝" x 2⅝"

From the coordinating floral print, cut:
- 6 squares, 5⅛" x 5⅛"

From the green print, cut:
- 4 strips, 4¼" x the lengthwise grain
- 4 binding strips, 2" x the lengthwise grain

From the remaining green print, cut:
- 6 squares, 5⅛" x 5⅛"
- 24 squares, 2⅝" x 2⅝"

From the yellow print, cut:
- 4 strips, 2" x 42"; crosscut into 68 squares, 2" x 2"

From the purple print, cut:
- 6 strips, 2" x 42"
- 14 strips, 2" x 42"; crosscut into 96 rectangles, 2" x 5⅜"

From the large-scale floral print, cut:
- 6 strips, 3" x 42"
- 11 strips, 2" x 42"; crosscut into 31 strips, 2" x 12½"
- 3 strips, 3⅞" x 42"; crosscut into 24 squares, 3⅞" x 3⅞"; cut each square once diagonally to yield 48 triangles

SEW-AND-TRIM TECHNIQUES

Making Flying-Geese Units (page 12)
Half-Square-Triangle Units (page 10)
Trimming Units with Crossed Seams (page 13)
Trimming Units to Make a Triangle (page 13)

MAKING THE BLOCKS

1. Sew two pink 2⅝" squares and a cream 2⅝" x 4¾" rectangle together to make a flying-geese unit; press. Make 24 units.

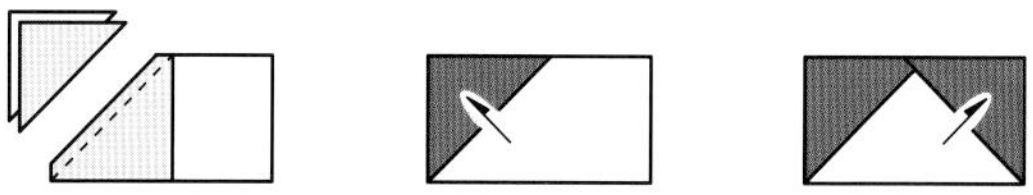

Make 24.

2. Draw a diagonal line from corner to corner on the wrong side of each coordinating floral 5⅛" square. Place a marked square on a green 5⅛" square, right sides together; stitch ¼" on each side of the drawn diagonal line. Cut and press toward the green triangle. Make 12 half-square-triangle units, each 4¾" x 4¾".

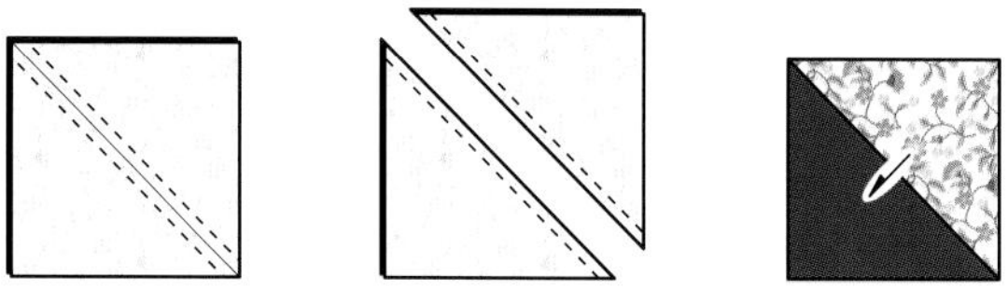

Make 12.

3. Sew a green 2⅝" square to one end of a cream 2⅝" x 4¾" rectangle to make a side unit. Press toward the green square. Make 24 side units.

Make 24.

4. Sew one cream 2⅝" square, one half-square-triangle unit from step 2, and two flying-geese units from step 1 together as shown; press. Make 12.

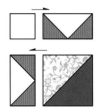

Make 12.

5. Sew two side units from step 3 to the unit from step 4 as shown; press. Trim the green squares, leaving a ¼" seam allowance beyond the crossed seams.

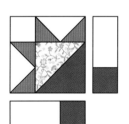 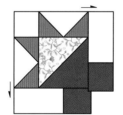

¼"

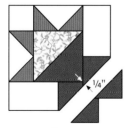

Make 12.

6. Fold a cream 5⅛" triangle in half and lightly press to mark the center of the long side. Sew the triangle to the unit from step 5, matching the center crease and the crossed seam. Press toward the cream triangle. Make 12 basket units.

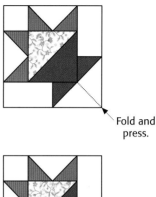

Fold and press.

Make 12.

7. Sew one yellow 2" square, two purple 2" x 5⅜" rectangles, and one large-scale floral 3⅞" triangle together as shown to make a corner unit. Press and trim the rectangles to create a 6⅞" triangle. Make 48.

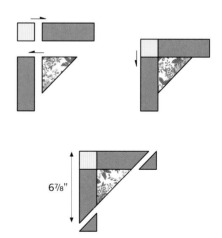

6⅞"

Make 48.

8. Fold a basket unit from step 6 in half vertically and horizontally and lightly crease to mark the center of each side. Fold four units from step 7 in half and lightly press to mark the center of the long side. Sew a unit from step 7 to opposite sides of a basket unit from step 6, matching the center creases; press. Sew a unit to the remaining sides of the basket unit to complete the block; press. Make 12.

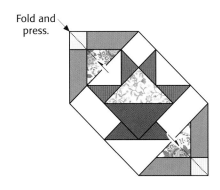

Fold and press.

Make 12.

QUILT TOP ASSEMBLY

1. Referring to "Assembling the Quilt Top" on pages 14–17, arrange the blocks and the 2" x 12½" large-scale floral sashing strips in rows. Sew four sashing strips and three blocks together to make a block row. Press the seams toward the sashing strips. Make four rows.

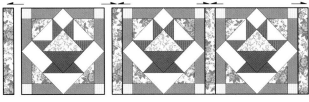

Make 4.

2. Sew four yellow 2" sashing squares and three 2" x 12½" large-scale floral sashing strips together to make a sashing row. Press the seams toward the sashing units. Make five rows.

Make 5.

3. Sew the block rows and sashing rows together. Press the seams toward the sashing rows.

ADDING THE BORDERS

For detailed instructions, refer to "Borders with Overlapped Corners" on pages 16–17.

1. Join the purple 2" inner-border strips end to end to make one continuous strip. Measure the quilt through the center from top to bottom and cut two border strips to fit that measurement.

2. Sew the trimmed inner-border strips to the side edges of the quilt top. Press toward the border strips.

3. Measure the quilt through the center from side to side, including the borders just added. Cut two purple 2" inner-border strips to fit that measurement.

4. Sew the 2" inner-border strips to the top and bottom edges of the quilt top. Press toward the border strips.

5. Repeat steps 1–4 to measure, trim, and add the large-scale floral print 3" middle-border strips. Press toward the border strips.

6. Repeat steps 1–4 to measure, trim, and add the green 4¼" outer-border strips. (You will not need to piece these strips.) Press toward the border strips.

FINISHING THE QUILT

For detailed instructions on finishing techniques, refer to "Finishing" on pages 18–22.

1. Cut and piece the backing fabric so it is 4" to 6" larger than the quilt top. Layer the quilt top with batting and backing. Baste the layers together.

2. Hand or machine quilt as desired.

3. Square up the quilt sandwich.

4. Using the green 2" strips, prepare and sew the binding to the quilt. Add a hanging sleeve, if desired, and a label.

Quilting suggestions: Quilt a medallion in the center of each basket block. Quilt in the ditch of the sashing and borders, and add a continuous design in the floral and green borders.

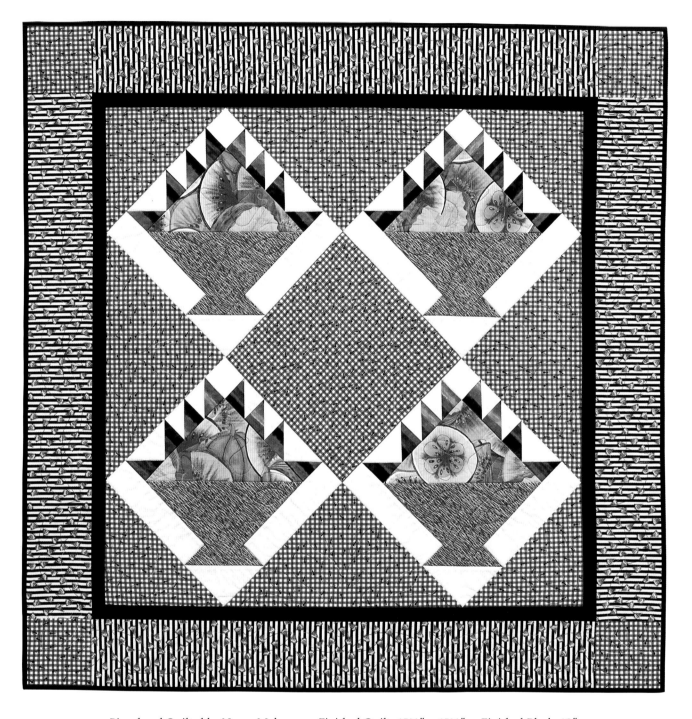

Pieced and Quilted by Nancy Mahoney · Finished Quilt: 45½" x 45½" · Finished Block: 12"

Capture the feeling of summer and memories of family picnics with this bright and cheery quilt. It's quick and easy and has only four blocks, so you can whip one up in no time. Hang it on a wall or use it on a table to add a little spice to any room.

MATERIALS

All yardages are based on 42"-wide fabric.

♦ 1 yard of pink check for setting square and triangles
♦ ¾ yard of black-and-white stripe for borders
♦ ⅝ yard of white tone-on-tone print for blocks
♦ ⅝ yard of black for borders and binding
♦ 1 fat quarter of green print for blocks
♦ 1 fat quarter of tan print for blocks
♦ 1 fat quarter of melon print for blocks
♦ 3 yards of fabric for backing
♦ 50" x 50" piece of batting

CUTTING

From the green print, cut:
♦ 8 squares, 2⅞" x 2⅞"
♦ 16 squares, 2½" x 2½"

From the white tone-on-tone print, cut:
♦ 2 strips, 2½" x 42"; crosscut into 8 rectangles, 2½" x 8½"
♦ 1 strip, 2½" x 42"; crosscut into 8 rectangles, 2½" x 4½"
♦ 1 strip, 2⅞" x 42"; crosscut into 8 squares, 2⅞" x 2⅞"
♦ 2 squares, 4⅞" x 4⅞"; cut once diagonally to yield 4 triangles
♦ 4 squares, 2½" x 2½"

From the melon print, cut:
♦ 2 squares, 8⅞" x 8⅞"

From the tan print, cut:
♦ 2 squares, 8⅞" x 8⅞"
♦ 8 squares, 2½" x 2½"

From the pink check, cut:
♦ 1 square, 18¾" x 18¾"; cut twice diagonally to yield 4 triangles
♦ 1 square, 12½ x 12½"
♦ 2 squares, 9¾" x 9¾"; cut once diagonally to yield 4 triangles
♦ 4 squares, 5" x 5"

From the black, cut:
♦ 5 binding strips, 2" x 42"
♦ 4 strips, 1½" x 42"

From the black-and-white stripe, cut:
♦ 4 strips, 5" x 42"

SEW-AND-TRIM TECHNIQUES

Making Flying-Geese Units (page 12)
Half-Square-Triangle Units (page 10)
Trimming Units with Crossed Seams (page 13)

MAKING THE BLOCKS

1. Sew two green 2½" squares and a white 2½" x 4½" rectangle together to make a flying-geese unit; press. Make eight units.

Make 8.

2. Draw a diagonal line from corner to corner on the wrong side of each white 2⅞" square. Place a marked white square on a green 2⅞" square, right sides together; stitch ¼" on each side of the drawn line. Cut and press. Make 16 half-square-triangle units, each 2½" x 2½".

Make 16.

3. Draw a diagonal line from corner to corner on the wrong side of each melon print 8⅞" square. Place a marked melon print square on each tan 8⅞" square, right sides together; stitch ¼" on each side of the drawn line. Cut and press. Make four half-square-triangle units, each 8½" x 8½".

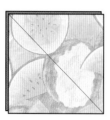

Make 4.

4. Sew a tan 2½" square to one end of a white 2½" x 8½" rectangle to make a side unit. Press toward the tan square. Make eight side units.

Make 8.

5. Sew two flying-geese units from step 1, four half-square-triangle units from step 2, one half-square-triangle unit from step 3, and one white 2½" square together as shown; press. Make four.

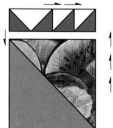

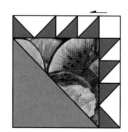

Make 4.

6. Sew two side units from step 4 to the unit from step 5 as shown; press. Trim the tan squares, leaving a ¼" seam allowance beyond the crossed seams. Make four.

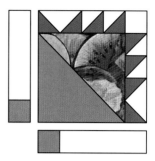

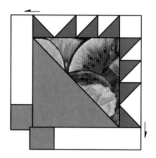

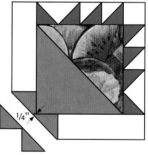

Make 4.

7. Fold a white 4⅞" triangle in half and lightly press to mark the center of the long side. Sew the triangle to the unit from step 6, matching the center crease and the crossed seam to complete one block. Press toward the white triangle. Make four blocks.

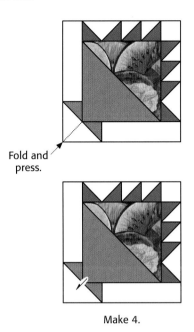

Fold and press.

Make 4.

QUILT TOP ASSEMBLY

1. Referring to "Assembling the Quilt Top" on pages 14–17, lay out the basket blocks and the pink check 12½" setting square. Add the pink check 18¾" side triangles.

2. Sew the blocks, setting square, and side triangles together in rows, pressing toward the pink check.

3. Sew the rows together, adding the pink check 9¾" corner triangles last. Press the seams toward the pink check.

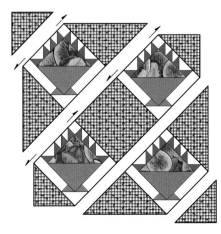

4. Square up the quilt top, trimming the edges ¼" from the corners of the blocks as needed.

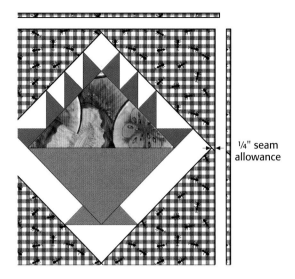

¼" seam allowance

ADDING THE BORDERS

For detailed instructions, refer to "Borders with Overlapped Corners" on pages 16–17.

1. Measure the quilt through the center from top to bottom and cut two black 1½" inner-border strips to fit that measurement.

2. Sew the trimmed inner-border strips to the side edges of the quilt top. Press toward the border strips.

3. Measure the quilt through the center from side to side, including the borders just added. Cut two black 1½" inner-border strips to fit that measurement.

4. Sew the trimmed inner-border strips to the top and bottom edges of the quilt top; press.

5. Measure the quilt through the center from top to bottom, including the inner-borders. Cut two striped 5" outer-border strips to fit that measurement.

6. Measure the quilt through the center from side to side, including the inner-borders. Cut two striped outer-border strips to fit that measurement.

7. Sew the trimmed striped outer-border strips from step 5 to the side edges of the quilt top. Press toward the border strips.

8. Sew a pink check 5" square to each end of the two remaining border strips. Press toward the border strips. Sew the border strips to the top and bottom edges of the quilt top; press.

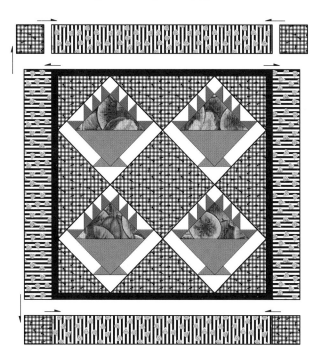

FINISHING THE QUILT

For detailed instructions on finishing techniques, refer to "Finishing" on pages 18–22.

1. Cut and piece the backing fabric so it is 4" to 6" larger than the quilt top. Layer the quilt top with batting and backing. Baste the layers together.

2. Hand or machine quilt as desired.

3. Square up the quilt sandwich.

4. Using the black 2" strips, prepare and sew the binding to the quilt. Add a hanging sleeve, if desired, and a label.

Quilting suggestions: Quilt each basket with a medallion in the large half-square-triangle unit in the center of the block. Quilt a medallion pattern in the large square and a partial medallion in the side and corner triangles. Quilt in the ditch around the black border and add a continuous design in the border.

Pieced and Quilted by Nancy Mahoney · Finished Quilt: 39¾" x 39¾" · Finished Block: 6"

I love this quilt—it looks whimsical and quirky, and it's so easy to make. The little red baskets and uneven nine-patch blocks just zoom together. It's practically guaranteed to brighten any room. Make one with a chicken print, and then make a second one with another favorite fabric!

MATERIALS

All yardages are based on 42"-wide fabric.

- 1 yard of chicken print for blocks, borders, and binding
- 1 yard of white tone-on-tone print for blocks
- ⅝ yard of red print for blocks and borders
- ½ yard of black print for blocks and borders
- 2⅝ yards of fabric for backing
- 44" x 44" piece of batting

CUTTING

From the red print, cut:

- 4 strips, 1⅛" x 42"
- 1 strip, 5⅛" x 42"; crosscut into 7 squares, 5⅛" x 5⅛"; cut each square once diagonally to yield 13 triangles (14 total; 1 is extra)
- 1 strip, 2⅝" x 42"; crosscut into 13 squares, 2⅝" x 2⅝"
- 2 strips, 1⅜" x 42"; crosscut into 13 rectangles, 1⅜" x 4¼"
- 2 strips, 1⅜" x 42"; crosscut into 13 rectangles, 1⅜" x 5⅛"

From the white tone-on-tone print, cut:

- 3 strips, 2" x 42"; crosscut 1 strip into 2 rectangles, 2" x 10"
- 1 strip, 3½" x 42"
- 1 strip, 3½" x 21"
- 3 strips, 3⅞" x 42"; crosscut into 26 squares, 3⅞" x 3⅞"; cut 13 squares once diagonally to yield 26 triangles (set the remaining 13 squares aside)
- 1 strip, 3⅜" x 42"; crosscut into 7 squares, 3⅜" x 3⅜"; cut each square once diagonally to yield 13 triangles (14 total; 1 is extra)

From the chicken print, cut:

- 5 strips, 3½" x 42"
- 1 rectangle, 3½" x 10"
- 5 binding strips, 2" x 42"

From the black print, cut:

- 4 strips, 1½" x 42"
- 3 strips, 2" x 42"; crosscut 1 strip into 2 strips, 2" x 21"

SEW-AND-TRIM TECHNIQUES

Trimming Units to Make a Triangle (page 13)
Making Units from Strip Sets (page 11)

MAKING THE BLOCKS

1. Using a pencil and ruler, draw a diagonal line from corner to corner on the wrong side of each red 2⅝" square. Place a marked red square on the corner of a white 3⅞" square, with right sides together and raw edges aligned. Stitch directly on the drawn diagonal line. Trim the corner, leaving a ¼" seam allowance. Press toward the red print. Make 13.

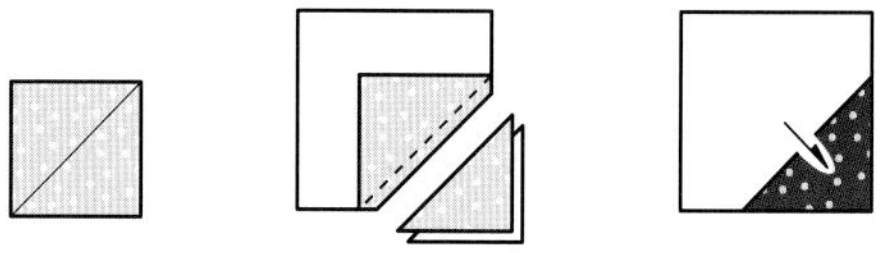

Make 13.

2. Using a ruler and rotary cutter, cut each square from step 1 on the diagonal to yield 13 triangle units and 13 reversed triangle units.

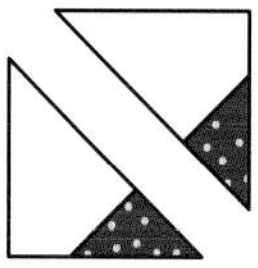

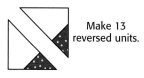

Make 13 reversed units.

Make 13 units.

3. Sew a white 3⅜" triangle, one red 1⅜" x 4¼" rectangle, and one red 1⅜" x 5⅛" rectangle together as shown. Press toward the red rectangles. Trim the rectangles to create a 5⅛" triangle. Make 13.

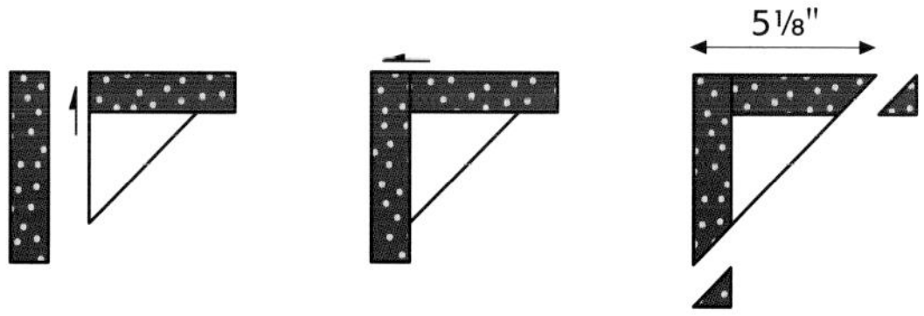

Make 13.

4. Sew a red 5⅛" triangle to the unit from step 2 as shown. Press toward the red triangle. Make 13.

Make 13.

5. Fold a unit from step 4 in half vertically and horizontally and lightly crease to mark the center of each side. Fold a reversed triangle unit from step 1 and a 3⅞" white triangle in half and lightly press to mark the center of the long side. Sew the triangles to the unit from step 4, matching the center creases. Fold a triangle unit from step 1 and a white 3⅞" triangle in half and lightly press to mark the center of the long side. Sew the triangles to the remaining sides to complete the block; press. Make 13 and label them block A.

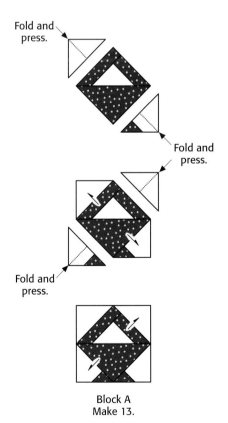

Block A
Make 13.

6. Sew two white 2" x 42" strips and one chicken print 3½" x 42" strip together to make strip set A. Sew two white 2" x 10" rectangles and one chicken print 3½" x 10" rectangle together to make a second strip set A. Press toward the chicken print strip. Cut the two strip sets into a total of 12 segments, each 3½" wide.

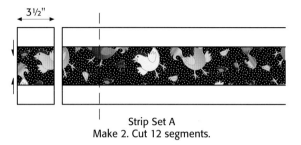

Strip Set A
Make 2. Cut 12 segments.

7. Sew two black 2" x 42" strips and the white 3½" x 42" strip together to make strip set B. Sew two black 2" x 21" strips and one white 3½" x 21" strip together to make a second strip set B. Press toward the black print. Cut the two strip sets into a total of 24 segments, each 2" wide.

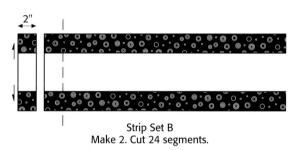

Strip Set B
Make 2. Cut 24 segments.

8. Sew two segments from strip set B and one segment from strip set A together to complete one block. Press as shown. Make 12 and label them block B.

Block B
Make 12.

QUILT TOP ASSEMBLY

1. Referring to "Assembling the Quilt Top" on pages 14–17, arrange the blocks in rows, alternating blocks A and B.

2. Sew the blocks together in rows, pressing the seams toward block B.

3. Sew the rows together, pressing the seam allowances in one direction.

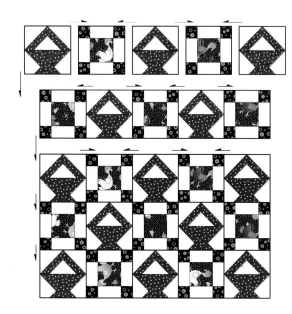

ADDING THE BORDERS

For detailed instructions, refer to "Borders with Overlapped Corners" on pages 16–17.

1. Measure the quilt through the center from top to bottom and cut two black 1½" inner-border strips to that measurement.

2. Sew the trimmed black inner-border strips to the side edges of the quilt top. Press toward the border strips.

3. Measure the quilt through the center from side to side, including the borders just added. Cut two black 1½" inner-border strips to that measurement.

4. Sew the trimmed inner-border strips to the top and bottom edges of the quilt top; press.

5. Repeat steps 1–4 to measure, trim, and add the red print 1⅛" middle border. Press toward the border strips.

6. Repeat steps 1–4 to measure, trim, and add the chicken print 3½" outer border; press.

FINISHING THE QUILT

For detailed instructions on finishing techniques, refer to "Finishing" on pages 18–22.

1. Cut and piece the backing fabric, if needed, so it is 4" to 6" larger than the quilt top. Layer the quilt top with batting and backing. Baste the layers together.

2. Hand or machine quilt as desired.

3. Square up the quilt sandwich.

4. Using the chicken print 2" strips, prepare and sew the binding to the quilt. Add a hanging sleeve, if desired, and a label.

Quilting suggestions: Quilt each Basket and Nine Patch block in the ditch. Add diagonal quilting lines to the black squares of the Nine Patch blocks. Quilt the borders with a continuous design and in the ditch.

Pieced and Quilted by Nancy Mahoney · Finished Quilt: 50½" x 50½" · Finished Blocks: 13¾", 10", and 7"

A medallion setting and three different basket blocks come together to make this striking quilt a winning combination. Here's your chance to showcase lavish quilting in the large triangles around the center block. The red-and-green color scheme is perfect for holiday decorating, or use red, white, and blue for a patriotic star.

MATERIALS

All yardages are based on 42"-wide fabric.

- 1⅝ yards of red floral print for blocks and borders
- 1⅝ yards of beige print for blocks and setting triangles
- 1⅜ yards of green print for blocks, borders, and binding
- 1 fat quarter of gold floral print for blocks
- 3⅜ yards of fabric for backing
- 55" x 55" piece of batting

CUTTING

From the beige print, cut:

- 1 strip, 3¼" x 42"; crosscut into 2 rectangles, 3¼" x 8¾", and 3 squares, 3¼" x 3¼"
- 1 strip, 3⅝" x 42"; crosscut into 5 squares, 3⅝" x 3⅝"
- 1 strip, 2½" x 42"; crosscut into 8 rectangles, 2½" x 4½"
- 2 strips, 2½" x 42"; crosscut into 8 rectangles, 2½" x 6½", and 4 squares, 2½" x 2½"
- 2 strips, 2¼" x 42"; crosscut into 16 rectangles, 2¼" x 4", and 4 squares, 2¼" x 2¼"
- 2 squares, 12" x 12"; cut once diagonally to yield 4 triangles
- 2 squares, 11¾" x 11¾"; cut twice diagonally to yield 8 triangles
- 1 square, 8" x 8"
- 1 square, 6⅜" x 6⅜"; cut once diagonally to yield 1 triangle (2 total; 1 is extra)
- 2 squares, 4⅞" x 4⅞"; cut once diagonally to yield 4 triangles
- 2 squares, 4⅜" x 4⅜"; cut once diagonally to yield 4 triangles

From the red floral print, cut:

- 4 strips, 4½" x the lengthwise grain

From the remaining red floral print, cut:

- 2 squares, 11¾" x 11¾"; cut twice diagonally to yield 8 triangles
- 1 square, 8" x 8"
- 5 squares, 3⅝" x 3⅝"
- 16 squares, 2½" x 2½"
- 16 squares, 2¼" x 2¼"

From the green print, cut:

- 6 binding strips, 2" x 42"
- 5 strips, 1½" x 42"
- 2 squares, 11¾" x 11¾"; cut twice diagonally to yield 8 triangles
- 1 square, 9⅛" x 9⅛"; cut once diagonally to yield 1 triangle (2 total; 1 is extra)
- 2 squares, 6⅞" x 6⅞"
- 2 squares, 4⅜" x 4⅜"
- 2 squares, 3¼" x 3¼"
- 8 squares, 2½" x 2½"
- 8 squares, 2¼" x 2¼"

From the gold floral print, cut:

- 2 squares, 6⅞" x 6⅞"
- 2 squares, 4⅜" x 4⅜"

SEW-AND-TRIM TECHNIQUES

Half-Square-Triangle Units (page 10)
Trimming Units with Crossed Seams (page 13)
Multiple Half-Square-Triangle Units (page 9)
Making Flying-Geese Units (page 12)

MAKING THE BLOCKS

1. Draw a diagonal line from corner to corner on the wrong side of each beige 3⅝" square. Place a marked beige square on a red 3⅝" square, right sides together; stitch ¼" on each side of the drawn line. Cut and press. Make ten half-square-triangle units, each 3¼" x 3¼".

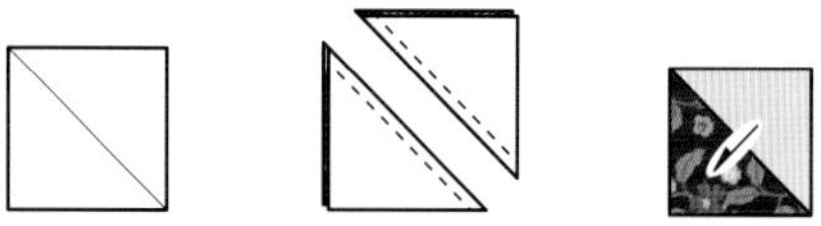

Make 10.

2. Sew three half-square-triangle units from step 1 and three beige 3¼" squares together in rows as shown; press. Sew the rows together; press. Trim away the excess fabric, leaving a ¼" seam allowance beyond the crossed seams. Make one.

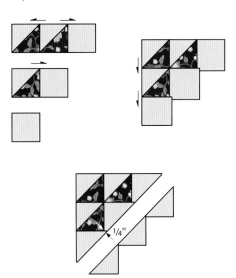

Make 1.

3. Sew the green 9⅛" triangle to the unit from step 2, pressing toward the green triangle. Make one.

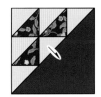

Make 1.

4. Sew seven half-square-triangle units from step 1 and the unit from step 3 together as shown; press. Make one.

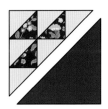
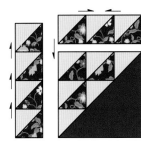
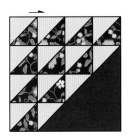

Make 1.

5. Sew a green 3¼" square to one end of a beige 3¼" x 8¾" rectangle to make a side unit. Press toward the green square. Make two side units.

Make 2.

6. Sew two side units from step 5 to the unit from step 4 as shown; press. Trim the green squares, leaving a ¼" seam allowance beyond the crossed seams. Make one.

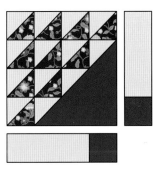

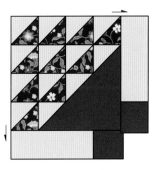

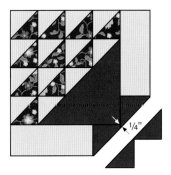

Make 1.

7. Fold the beige 6⅜" triangle in half and lightly press to mark the center of the long side. Sew the triangle to the unit from step 6, matching the center crease and the crossed seam to complete one block. Press toward the beige triangle. Make one and label it block A.

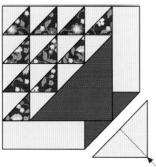

Fold and press.

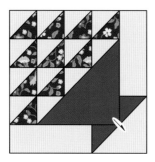

Block A
Make 1.

8. Pair the red 8" square with the beige 8" square, right sides facing up. Cut and piece 2½"-wide bias strips. Make two strip sets. Cut eight half-square-triangle units, each 2½" x 2½".

Make 2 strip sets.
Cut 8 units.

9. Sew two red 2½" squares and one beige 2½" x 4½" rectangle together to make a flying-geese unit; press. Make eight units.

Make 8.

10. Draw a diagonal line from corner to corner on the wrong side of both gold 6⅞" squares. Place a gold square on a green 6⅞" square, right sides together; stitch ¼" on each side of the drawn line. Cut and press. Make four half-square-triangle units, each 6½" x 6½".

Make 4.

11. Sew a green 2½" square to one end of a beige 2½" x 6½" rectangle to make a side unit. Press toward the green square. Make eight side units.

Make 8.

12. Sew one beige 2½" square, two half-square-triangle units from step 8, two units from step 9, and one half-square-triangle unit from step 10 together as shown; press. Make four.

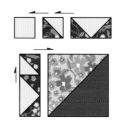 

Make 4.

13. Sew two side units from step 11 to the unit from step 12 as shown; press. Trim the green squares, leaving a ¼" seam allowance beyond the crossed seams. Make four.

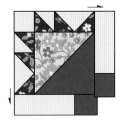
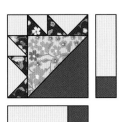

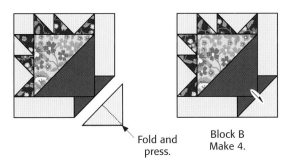

Make 4.

14. Repeat step 7 to sew a beige 4⅞" triangle to the unit from step 13 to complete one block; press. Make four and label them block B.

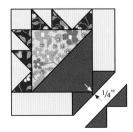

Fold and press.

Block B
Make 4.

15. Sew two red 2¼" squares and one beige 2¼" x 4" rectangle together to make a flying-geese unit; press. Make eight units.

Make 8.

16. Repeat step 10, placing a marked gold 4⅜" square on a green 4⅜" square to make four half-square-triangle units, each 4" x 4".

Make 4.

17. Sew a green 2¼" square to one end of a beige 2¼" x 4" rectangle to make a side unit. Press toward the green square. Make eight side units.

Make 8.

18. Sew one beige 2¼" square, one half-square-triangle unit from step 16, and two flying-geese units from step 15 together as shown; press. Make four.

Make 4.

19. Sew two side units from step 17 to the unit from step 18 as shown; press. Trim the green squares, leaving a ¼" seam allowance beyond the crossed seams. Make four.

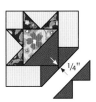

Make 4.

20. Repeat step 7 to sew a beige 4⅜" triangle to the unit from step 19; press. Make four blocks and label them block C.

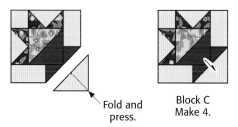

Fold and press.

Block C
Make 4.

QUILT TOP ASSEMBLY

1. Fold block A in half vertically and horizontally and lightly crease to mark the center of each side. Fold the four beige 12" triangles in half and lightly crease to mark the center of the long side. Sew a triangle to opposite sides of block A, matching the center creases; press. Sew a triangle to the remaining sides of the block to complete the center unit; press.

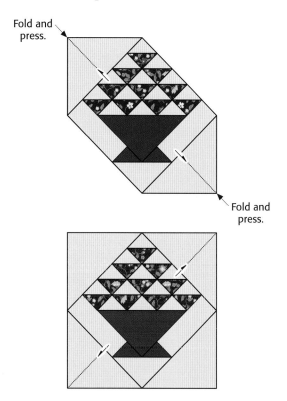

Fold and press.

Fold and press.

2. Square up the center unit to 20½" x 20½". The distance from the corners of the block will be approximately ⅜", depending on the size of your block. The block may "float" a bit—the points may not be precisely at the seam after it is sewn to

the next units. This is fine, as long as the block is centered and the overall dimensions of the center unit measure 20½" x 20½", including seam allowances, after the excess fabric is trimmed.

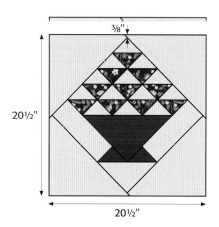

3. Arrange and sew two beige, two red, and two green 11¾" triangles and one block C together to make each side unit as shown. Position the triangles so that all the baskets remain upright in the quilt layout. Press as shown. Make two horizontal units and two vertical units. Square up each unit, trimming the edges ¼" from the corners of the blocks as needed. The side units should measure 10½" x 20½", including seam allowances.

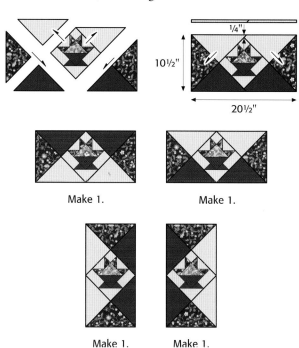

Make 1.   Make 1.

Make 1.   Make 1.

4. Arrange and sew the center unit from step 2, two horizontal side units from step 3, two vertical side units from step 3, and four B blocks in rows as shown. Press as shown. Sew the rows together and press.

ADDING THE BORDERS

For detailed instructions, refer to "Borders with Overlapped Corners" on pages 16–17.

1. Join the green 1½" inner-border strips end to end to make one continuous strip. Measure the quilt through the center from top to bottom and cut two border strips to fit that measurement.

2. Sew the trimmed inner-border strips to the side edges of the quilt top. Press toward the border strips.

3. Measure the quilt through the center from side to side, including the borders just added. Cut two green 1½" border strips to fit that measurement.

4. Sew the trimmed inner-border strips to the top and bottom edges of the quilt top. Press toward the border strips.

5. Repeat steps 1–4 to measure, trim, and add the red 4½" outer border. (You will not need to piece the strips.) Press toward the border strips.

FINISHING THE QUILT

For detailed instructions on finishing techniques, refer to "Finishing" on pages 18–22.

1. Cut and piece the backing fabric so it is 4" to 6" larger than the quilt top. Layer the quilt top with batting and backing. Baste the layers together.

2. Hand or machine quilt as desired.

3. Square up the quilt sandwich.

4. Using the green 2" strips, prepare and sew the binding to the quilt. Add a hanging sleeve, if desired, and a label.

Quilting suggestions: Quilt medallion designs and partial medallions as shown. Quilt in the ditch around the inner border and stitch a continuous feather design in the outer border.

Nancy Mahoney is an enthusiastic quiltmaker, author, teacher, and fabric designer. She enjoys speaking at quilt guilds and meeting other quilters, especially beginners. This is Nancy's fourth book with Martingale & Company.

Nancy has been actively quilting since 1987, and since then her quilts have been featured in many quilt books and national quilt magazines. Nancy's quilts have won many awards, including two first-place ribbons. She enjoys the art of quiltmaking and believes that each quilt is a fun and exciting learning experience. She likes to use traditional blocks to create quilts that look complex but are easy to make using updated techniques.

Nancy lives in Palm Coast, Florida. When she's not quilting, she enjoys gardening, walking on the beach, and shopping for antiques.